COACHING

Jim San Marco
AND
Kurt Aschermann

Foreword by Julio Mazzei

KIDS
TO PLAY
SOCCER

A FIRESIDE BOOK

Published by Simon & Schuster

NEW YORK   LONDON   TORONTO   SYDNEY   TOKYO

OTHER BOOKS
(by Kurt Aschermann and Gerard P. O'Shea)

Coaching Kids to Play Baseball and Softball

Permission to reprint USSF soccer rules courtesy United States Soccer Federation.

Glossary terms and definitions used by permission of the Ontario Soccer Association—from their Schools Programme Manual.

A Fireside Book

Published by Simon & Schuster, Inc.

Rockefeller Center
1230 Avenue of the Americas
New York, New York 10020

FIRESIDE and colophon are registered trademarks of
Simon & Schuster, Inc.

Designed by Stanley S. Drate/Folio Graphics Co., Inc.

Manufactured in the United States of America

20   19   18   17   16   15   14   13   12

Library of Congress Cataloging in Publication Data

San Marco, Jim.
  Coaching kids to play soccer.

  "A Fireside book."
  Includes index.
  1. Soccer for children—Coaching. I. Aschermann,
Kurt. II. Title.
GV943.8.S26   1987   796.334′024054   87-8544
ISBN: 0-671-63936-6

DEDICATION

This book is dedicated to: Lou Gallo and Frank Chillemi,
who started my soccer life; Mario and Ann, my parents,
who gave me my life; Skip, Johnny, Deb and Fran, who
have been such a big part of my life; Lesley, my wife, who
has with great love and patience shared my life; Mary and
Jill, my children, who each day help me to appreciate life;
and finally, to God, the most important thing in my life.

—JIM SAN MARCO

This book is dedicated to my wife, Laura, who has made
everything and anything I have done for the past 11 years
possible and whose dedication, faith and love have given
me the courage, strength and willingness to try new things
and usually succeed at them.

—KURT ASCHERMANN

We would like to thank our soccer players whose pictures
appear throughout the book:
  Jennifer Aschermann
  Kurt Aschermann
  Kristin Aschermann
  Mary San Marco
  Jill San Marco
  Geoff Simone

CONTENTS

FOREWORD

Soccer's development in the United States has been swift. Today we see thousands of kids playing the sport seven days a week, twelve months a year.

When I came to this country twelve years ago with the legendary Pelé, some soccer was being played by children. It was, however, to a great extent unorganized, and often the coaches were untrained and ill-prepared to teach the correct skills and techniques. Today, coaches' training has improved dramatically. We are beginning to see our young people become better skilled in this, the sport Pelé called "the beautiful game."

Because soccer is still relatively new to this country, however, the need for instructional tools continues. This book, *Coaching Kids to Play Soccer*, goes a long way toward answering this need. Jim San Marco and Kurt Aschermann have combined their substantial experience in the game, and in youth sports in general, into a concise yet detailed guidebook. With this book, the youth soccer coach can plan a worthwhile season of fun and learning for the young people of America involved in the world's most popular sport.

The specific soccer details in this book make it a welcome addition to any soccer coach's library. But just as

9

important, a positive philosophy of coaching young people informs its every page. The authors' attitude that the player must always come first does much, I think, to encourage the total development of the player.

Professor Julio Mazzei
  Director of Pelé USA-Brazil Soccer Tournament
  Former Coach of the N.Y. Cosmos
  The Winningest Coach in NASL History

PREFACE

Just how many kids are there in America playing soccer? Estimates vary, but the quantified analysis is really irrelevant. Suffice it to say there are *lots* of kids playing this game the rest of the world calls football. An afternoon's ride through Long Island in New York, or the suburbs of St. Louis or Los Angeles, will prove the point. One can see youngsters of every shape, size, color and sex, kicking that round thing from one end of a field to another.

The proponents of soccer development in the United States will tell you it's an American game because all kinds of people live here and anyone can play soccer. Others contend that the game takes no skill—it's just a bunch of kids kicking each other's shins.

The purpose of this book is *not* to try to convince anyone of anything. We want to state, however, that we slip into the first category—we love the sport of soccer, we see what it's done for millions of kids, and we want to see its continued growth. But we also believe that soccer people spend too much time "preaching" the virtues of the sport, and not enough time "teaching" them. They need to abandon the argument altogether and get on with the sport's development.

A point often made pertaining to soccer is: with so many kids playing it, how come you can't get them to watch it played professionally? We have some thoughts on the matter, but quite frankly, we don't lose sleep over it. You won't find the answer to that question in this book.

This book, then, is simply to help the volunteer or first-time coach learn the game and advise how best to teach it. It is written as if that person knows nothing at all about soccer (a safe bet, in most cases).

In 1984, Kurt Aschermann co-authored a very successful baseball instructional book entitled *Coaching Kids to Play Baseball and Softball*, a companion to this book. In the preface it was said, "This book is for you, the volunteer coach or parent who loves the game of baseball and enjoys working with youngsters, but may need some assistance in teaching the sport effectively and enjoyably. It's a book of basics, not a detailed skill level book."

This book, *Coaching Kids to Play Soccer*, is the same type of manual. We have combined our administrative, coaching and soccer experience into a guidebook for the volunteer coach. You won't find esoteric descriptions of elaborate defenses and strategy in these pages. What you *will* find is all the information you need to coach the likes of second-grade "Kipp's Pharmacy Raiders," a 14-year-old select team, or a junior varsity squad at your local high school, and thus enjoy with them what is truly the world's most popular sport.

The authors come from different backgrounds. Kurt Aschermann is currently President of Kurlar Associates, a firm that specializes in sports education and instruction programs and consults to corporate, public and private recreation agencies. Though Aschermann was a high school baseball coach for five years, he has little experience coaching soccer, serving principally as a coach for five-, six-, and seven-year-olds. He has extensive youth sports experience and is considered an expert in the field of volunteer youth athletics.

Jim San Marco, a past president of the Westchester County Soccer Coaches Association, is one of the most successful high school soccer coaches in New York State.

His Edgemont High School (Westchester County) soccer teams have won their sectional cup in 1983, 1984 and 1985; and his combined record in 13 years of coaching is an incredible 158-46-21. He has worked with volunteer soccer associations and serves as a commissioner of an AYSO junior league in his home town. A noted soccer clinician, San Marco coached a team in 1986 in the North American Junior Maccabi Games.

COACHING
KIDS
TO PLAY
SOCCER

1

IT'S ALL YOURS, COACH

A simple, important, sobering fact needs to be stated at the outset: as a youth soccer coach you have a huge responsibility to everyone on the team. Not only do these youngsters want to learn soccer from you, but they also want to win, want to score some goals—and they don't want to be yelled at. Your impact is rivaled only by that of the parent, and in certain circumstances, it surpasses that influence. You will find that your kids want to please you more than anyone else, and this simple fact can place tremendous pressure on you. It should guide your every action.

We believe that your responsibilities as a youth soccer coach are easily stated:

Fun
Learning
Individual development
Winning

. . . in that order! Let's look at each one in turn:

Fun: It may come as a surprise to some of the parents of the players, but 99 percent of the kids are playing soccer because they want to have fun playing it. Those kids in your charge, Coach, have joined the league and your team to enjoy themselves. The minute you lose sight of that as your principal motivating factor, you're in trouble.

Learning: Youth soccer coaches must be responsible, dedicated teachers—more so than other youth league coaches—because most kids in America don't know the sport! They grow up *catching the things that are thrown or kicked at them*, except for an occasional kickball. "Offside" is when the offensive guard (in football) moves before the ball is snapped. Couple player ignorance of soccer with magnified parental ignorance, Coach, and you can see why we put learning second on the list.

Individual Development: A nine-year-old should be compared with himself, not every other nine-year-old. You help a team develop by helping each individual. And if you've succeeded in helping most of your athletes become better soccer players by the last week of the season, you're a winning coach, regardless of your record.

Winning: We believe the outcome of the game yields winners and learners—there are no losers. Winning is important and needs to be an important part of the development of soccer players. But perspective becomes the important consideration, because while winning is important and must be part of the education process of an athlete, it needs to be understood as the result of hard work and individual development. The coach who succeeds in teaching the sport—individually and to a group—will find success in the won/lost column. The coach who helps the team keep winning or losing in perspective will find success in the personal development column.

THE BALL STOPS HERE

Coaches in volunteer leagues are often acquired like goalies: no one wants to do the job, especially, so someone gets drafted. You may have come to your soccer duties purely out of love for the sport or, like many, out of love for your child. Any coach, regardless of experience, has two factors that must be dealt with quickly: (1) individual knowledge of the sport and (2) ability to impart that knowledge to the youngsters. If you have come to your soccer team because your child wanted to play and no one else was there to teach or lead the team, how you deal with the two factors may well determine if the players have a positive or a negative experience.

2
GENERAL GUIDELINES FOR PARENTS, PLAYERS, AND COACHES

To avoid disagreements, frustration, and questions of proper conduct, it is necessary to state clearly what roles parents, players, and coaches play in organized soccer. Each group should understand the philosophy of the league, and if they wish to participate, they must follow the rules for the league. Following are some basic, common-sense expectations of parents, players, and coaches about to become involved in youth soccer:

PARENTS

1. The primary reason children play is to have fun, not so much to win or to be with their friends.

2. Demand that your child play fairly, within the rules of the game.
3. Help the coaches in any way possible. Remember, they're volunteers and usually parents, too.
4. Don't make negative comments to any child, especially your own. Understand that when one of the players makes a mistake, he didn't do it on purpose; your method of correction should reflect that.

5. Praise the effort of every player; remember, the lesser skilled players are just as important as the superstars.
6. Be a parent who leads by example. Don't say one thing and do another.

PLAYERS

1. Always play fairly within the rules.
2. Maintain poise under difficult conditions. It's very easy to maintain composure when things go right; when they don't, real athletes step forward and stand up to the test.
3. Control your emotions, even if you feel your opponent is playing unfairly.
4. Support and encourage your teammates at all times. Any mistakes they make are surely not done on purpose.
5. Play as hard as you can in practice and games. Don't let your teammates down because of your lack of effort.
6. Show respect to your coaches and referees. Without them you would not be playing the game.

COACHES

1. Kids play soccer to have fun, so any decision you make concerning them should reflect that.
2. Be a knowledgeable coach. Read about soccer; discuss soccer with other coaches; go to clinics. You must know what you're talking about.
3. Demand that your players play within the rules of the game. If they win dishonestly, they haven't won at all.
4. Set a positive example for your players. Respect isn't given to anyone; it must be earned.
5. The safety of your players must be a priority. Don't take chances with their health or well-being. Winning the game means little when compared to overall safety.
6. Respect the opposing team and the referees, whether you approve of their actions or not.

3

PRE-PRACTICE PREPARATION (What Do I Do First?)

Many things must be done when planning the first practice session to assure that the proper tone is set and that you accomplish your objectives (let alone control the troops!)

After you have received a roster of the players, it's a good idea to send a letter to their parents explaining your view of soccer in general terms. Let them know what you will be doing at practices and in games. Mention immediate as well as long-range goals and what you expect from them and the children. In this way, no one should be surprised by anything that occurs during the season.

Your letter should include: (1) what each player needs to bring to the first practice; (2) when practice will take place and how long it will last; (3) a practice schedule, as well as a game schedule, to accommodate any long-range plans; (4) a phone chain and refreshment schedule for the team; and (5) some information about yourself—your background, family and soccer experience.

A sample letter follows:

Dear Parents:

Welcome to the Juniors' Soccer Program! We begin playing on Saturday, September 20, at the old middle school field. Practices will run from September 20 through November 1, from ten to eleven o'clock.

We will not be traveling and competing against other communities. Instead, our playing will be geared toward having FUN, taking fruit-punch breaks, socializing with kindergarten friends, chasing butterflies, and, if our children will cooperate a little, learning about the game of soccer. As parents, we are well aware of the attention span and physical limitations of our children. This program is not about to make polished soccer players out of four- and five-year-olds. First, it would be impossible and, second, it would be a frustrating situation for everyone included if we tried to do that. Instead, it is my hope that the kids will have fun, become a bit more fit, learn about themselves and others as they play together. I hope to accomplish these things through the game of soccer. We will be instructing the children in the basic rules of the game and the fundamental skills of the sport as we try to reach our goals.

The following are some important things you should know:

1. Your child may wear sneakers or cleats, and we require that he/she also wear shinguards.
2. We will be using a Size 3 soccer ball, smaller than the official Size 5, which will put less strain on the legs. Purchasing a Size 3 ball would prove a worthy investment for your child. Please try to bring a ball (with your name on it) to practice. We will do some exercises where each youngster will need a ball. At present we have 20 balls for the 24 children in the program.
3. Please be prompt when dropping off or picking up your child at the practices. Practice will last for one hour only.
4. If your child wears eyeglasses, be certain that the lenses are shatterproof or plastic. If they are not, have your child wear an eyeglass protective mask.
5. I have asked a few parents to help serve in a telephone chain in case inclement weather causes us to cancel a practice. If there is any doubt in your mind and you have not been called, just contact me at 123-4567.
6. Seven parents have volunteered to coach our children. We encourage you to join us at our practices, to help or just to watch. The more assistance we have at each practice, the more individual attention each child will receive.

Please call me if you have any questions or comments.

Thanks in advance,
Jim San Marco

TELEPHONE CHAIN

CAPTAINS

Joe Smith	123-4567	WILL CALL	Mary Jones	890-1234
			Ann Smith	567-8901
John Doe	234-5678	WILL CALL	Sue Johnson	901-2345
			Jane Hansen	678-9012
Lynn James	345-6789	WILL CALL	Ann S. John	012-3456
			Bill Joseph	789-0123
Mary Mason	456-7890	WILL CALL	Bob Johns	123-4567
			Sue Jones	890-1234
Jane Deer	567-8901	WILL CALL	Alice Smith	234-5678
			Ann Winters	901-2345
Wanda Simke	678-9012	WILL CALL	Al Frump	345-6789
			Sue Stein	012-3456
Al Lance	789-0123	WILL CALL	Jeff Jones	476-7890
			Jean James	123-4567

JIM SAN MARCO, 555-1234, will make the initial call to the captains to start the chain.

JOE SHOE has been kind enough to organize the water and punch-break schedule. PLEASE DO YOUR PART TO HELP.

PRACTICE SCHEDULE: SATURDAYS ONLY 10:00 A.M.–11:00 A.M.

SEPTEMBER	20
SEPTEMBER	27
OCTOBER	4
OCTOBER	11
OCTOBER	18
OCTOBER	25
NOVEMBER	1

On the first day of practice you should be at least fifteen to twenty minutes early, allowing you time to check for any problems with the field or anything else, and to try to resolve them. (You'd be surprised at some of the things first-time coaches have found on Day One!)

Set up equipment for your first practice exercise beforehand. This will save time later on. As the youngsters and parents arrive, welcome them and introduce yourself. (The parents, remember, are leaving a prized possession with you; they deserve to meet you right away.) Briefly state your expectations of the players and the scheduled season, touching as well on how you hope to meet these expectations if they will but do their best, help one another, never give up competing, and so forth.

After you talk, loosen up your players with *running and stretching* as you start practice. You will have quite a few appropriate exercises to use after reading this book.

As practice gets under way, you will begin a mental evaluation of the players in order to help determine what particular practice is needed most. The evaluation sheet shown on page 29 will help you assess each player's strengths and weaknesses. Obviously, it's a tool. You may or may not want to share it with the individual player.

As part of your preparation for the first practice, it is important for you to have a working knowledge of first-aid procedures. Any vigorous activity increases the possibility of injury, so it's imperative that you do everything you can to ensure the safety of your players. A first-aid course which can usually be taken in one day, is strongly recommended. (In many states, such a course is mandatory in order to coach a high school team.) The time spent learning proper procedures is just as important as the time taken to read this book. Do it—you won't regret it.

CONDUCTING A MEANINGFUL PRACTICE

Trust us on this one, Coach: **There is nothing more boring in the entire world of sport than a poorly planned and run practice.** You can literally waste the entire practice time if you don't know what you're going to do every minute *before* you get there.

There are some simple rules to follow when planning your practices that we feel guarantee that your time with your players will be quality time:

1. Never try to do too much. If you try to put in your offense, defense, and goal kick strategy on the same day, you will only succeed in confusing your players.

2. Teach one skill at a time. It's hard enough for little folks to understand one skill at a time; if you try to do more than one, they'll have trouble deciding which one to work on the most.

3. You must be able to demonstrate the new skill. This means that if you aren't skilled enough to actually show what you mean, you must have someone ready who is.

4. After you've taught it, try it. Many coaches teach a skill, then move on to another. Try it while it's still fresh in mind.

5. After trying it, add some pressure. It's always a good idea to let your players try a new skill with someone trying to stop them. GAME-RELATED PRESSURE, which obviously better approximates what they will feel in a contest, can be added as proficiency increases.

6. After teaching and trying, review it again. Reinforcement is important. The best time to do that is right after you have spent time on the skill.

7. Make it fun, fast-paced and frequently changed. Practice *has to be fun* or you won't accomplish much. By changing the activity and keeping things moving, you will find less boredom in the ranks and more learning.

A SAMPLE PRACTICE OUTLINE

Though no two practice sessions will be exactly alike, they should all be structured basically the same. Following is a general outline which details the steps to take for meaningful practice:

1. Start with a meeting at which you explain what you will do that day. It's also a good time to talk about past practices or even a game just played.

2. The warmup described in Chapter 15 is essential as the next step.

3. Teach new skills first. The best time for learning is when players are freshest and the most eager. That's at the start of practice.

4. Exercises for the new skill taught are next.

5. Exercises with some pressure follow.

6. Reviewing what was just taught helps reinforce the lesson.

7. Every practice should include *team-related* activities. Your offensive and defensive tactics and restarts should be worked on by the entire team after individual skills.

8. Every practice should have some gamelike work. Actual scrimmage, or even half-field scrimmages, are fun and kids look forward to them. Include them in every practice, but put them at the end. To many youngsters, scrimmage is the thing they come to practice for. If you scrimmage in the beginning, you may just lose them for the rest of practice.

9. A cool-down period at the end of practice is important. We'll talk more about this later in the book.

10. Finish each practice with a meeting. It's at this time that you will review what you've just accomplished and talk about what is coming up. The next game or practice schedule should be touched upon at this time, too, as well as anything else you want your players to remember. It's a good idea to bring the parents in on this one also.

SUMMARY

The well organized and run practice is essential to a good soccer program. The little time you take to *prepare* will be well worth your while in the long run.

PLAYER SKILL EVALUATION SHEET

If you had just received a promotion and were moving into a new office as boss, you would quickly evaluate the talent or skills of your employees. As a soccer coach you must do likewise with your players.

After a few practices with the kids, sit down with your assistant coaches and evaluate the players. Mark down what you perceive to be their weaknesses and strengths. This will help you set individual and team goals. Each practice should provide all players with a chance to work on their weaknesses. At the end of the season reevaluate your players; show them how they have improved and where you think they can improve more.

The form below provides a simple recording and evaluation system:

   CODE: 1—Skilled player
   2—Player has some skill
   3—Player has little skill

NAME	PASSING	SHOOTING LT/RT	RECEIVING	HEADING	DRIBBLING

EVALUATING HOW YOUR PLAYERS MOVE

This may surprise you, Coach, but most kids don't
know how to run. That's right, run. Oh, they know how to
get from one place to another quickly, but we guarantee
you that most of them have poor mechanics in their
running style. We believe that evaluating how they run

before you start your season, then working on improving the mechanics in running, will pay off in the long run.

Here's the things you want to look for in running style:

1. Elbows should be close to the body while the arms are pumping. Elbows that fly add unneeded movement that will slow the body down.

2. Knees should be brought straight up, causing the thighs to be parallel to the ground. Feet and thighs can fly away from the body, causing extra wind resistance and a slowed-down player.

3. Hands and legs should be *pumped* vigorously when running.

4. Players should lean slightly forward when running. (That's why sprinters lean forward when they run.)

5. Lateral movement is important to the game and must be evaluated and taught as well. Remember, kids move sideways in sports almost as much as forward and backward.

6. Ability to run backward is important also in soccer. It too must be evaluated and taught.

You may want to add a small line on your evaluation sheet where you can indicate which players need work on movement. But remember, all players need to work on movement and it should be part of your practices.

4

25 IMPORTANT THINGS YOUR PLAYERS SHOULD KNOW

1. A good soccer player must have skills, conditioning, and tactical knowledge. A player must work on all three to be the best he/she can be.
2. When your team has the ball, *everyone* is on offense; when your opponents have the ball, *everyone* is on defense.
3. A soccer team does not have backs, midfielders or strikers—only *soccer players*. No matter what position you may start the game in, you will still have to head, pass, receive, shoot, make space, etc., as any player would do regardless of position.
4. If you can't pass and receive a soccer ball, you can't play soccer. Practice passing to a man or to space with proper pace and receiving ground and air balls.
5. Do not just kick the ball unless it is in a dangerous position in front of our goal. Instead, take a "picture" of the situation *before* you get the ball. In this way you can perceive the situation, determine the best solution, and act accordingly when the ball arrives.
6. Don't run forward when your team has the ball, unless you run back when the other team has the ball.

7. You are limited in what your team can do by your players' skill.
8. In most sports you need to be balanced on both feet. In soccer, you must also have superior balance (to shoot, pass, receive, etc.) on *one foot*. The best way to develop and improve balance on one foot is by juggling.
9. If you lose the ball, you should be the first person on defense. Giving immediate chase is the first rule of defense.
10. When changing from offense to defense, sprint to get between your man and the goal you are defending.
11. Beat your opponent to the ball. It is more difficult for your opponent to score a goal if he doesn't have the ball.
12. If your opponent has the ball and his back is to you, *do not let him turn* with the ball or he can pass or dribble forward or shoot.
13. After a goal, always thank your teammate for the assist. Quite often that player has made the tougher play.
14. Never criticize the goalie after a goal: Before the ball got by him, ten players also let the ball get by them.
15. In a soccer game, only one team plays soccer. The other team chases. What would you like to do? Maintain possession of the ball!
16. Good dribblers give up the ball before they are in trouble, not *after* they are in trouble.
17. Losing possession of the ball is acceptable in three situations: after a goal, after a shot, or in the offensive third of the field.
18. *Do not say anything to a referee!* They are not *dishonest*, but sometimes they will make mistakes, just as we do.
19. If all of your players made as few mistakes as referees in a game, the team would be undefeated every season.
20. To play up to your ability, you cannot smoke, drink, or take drugs.
21. An effort of 99 percent or less will not win championships or ball games against good competition.

22. The world is full of potentially good soccer players, but lacking in players that *reach* that potential.
23. Potential means that you haven't done anything yet.
24. Players should not be allowed to say "I can't" or give excuses. "I'll try" will be accepted.
25. Win, lose, or tie, if you have given 100 percent when you walk off the field, you have nothing to be ashamed of and should not have any regrets.

Okay, we hear you: "These sound great, but what do they mean?" Read on and find out!

5

THE RULES OF THE GAME AND DIMENSIONS OF THE FIELD

We can hear you now: "What kind of sports instruction book puts rules of the game in the middle of the book? It belongs at the end." Nope, not for soccer. We know that sports books traditionally put the rules at the end, but we think they belong here, early on, because in many cases, assigned coaches *don't know them*. Additionally, lots of good, pertinent advice and instruction may be found right within these rules.

We are giving the rules from the United States Soccer Federation verbatim because we think they best describe the game itself in easy-to-understand fashion. But be aware that most youth leagues *adapt* the rules of soccer to accommodate the size of the players or the size of their fields. *Make sure you know the rules of your league before you start*. It's not productive to warn or drill your players on the penalty for a bad throw in being loss of possession, only to find that your league allows another try. Read the USSF's Rules and your own league's rules carefully.

There are 17 laws, or rules, of soccer as laid down by the ruling body of soccer, FIFA. These provide guidelines for playing the game. The laws are simple, flexible, yet specific. It is the responsibility of the coach to know and understand these laws thoroughly and to pass this knowledge on to the players. In addition to maintaining the spirit of the laws, the coach must be concerned with their tactical application. He can use them to his team's advantage, while staying within their limits. The brief commentary that follows the summary of each law suggests ways in which to do this.

LAW I. THE FIELD OF PLAY
The soccer field is rectangular, its length not more than 130 yards nor less than 100 yards and its width not more than 100 yards nor less than 50 yards. At each end are a goal, a goal area, and a penalty area with a penalty spot. In addition, the field is marked with a center circle, center spot, penalty arcs, corner areas, and a halfway line. Flags are placed at each corner of the field and, optionally, just outside each touchline, or sideline, opposite the halfway line.

Commentary: Depending on the broad characteristics of a team, the size of the field can be an asset or a liability. A very fit, fast team with mediocre technique will be more effective on a large field. On the other hand, a slower, less fit team with excellent technical skills will perform better on a small field.

LAW II. THE BALL
The ball is made of leather or other approved material. Its circumference is between 27 and 28 inches and the weight, at the start of the game, between 14 and 16 ounces. The ball cannot be changed during a game without the referee's permission.

Commentary: The size, weight, air pressure, and material of the ball should be determined by the skill levels of the players. Players with poor skills will find it easier to control a big, heavy ball inflated to minimum pressure. Youth players should use smaller balls. The balls used in practice should be the same as those used in games.

LAW III. NUMBER OF PLAYERS
Teams have 11 players, one of whom is the goalkeeper. Any of the field players may change places with the goalkeeper, provided the referee is informed of the switch and the change is made during a stoppage of play. In international competition no more than 2 substitutes are allowed, but in other matches up to 5 substitutes may be allowed as long as the 2 teams agree on the number beforehand and inform the referee prior to the match. The referee must be informed of all substitutions, and once replaced, a player may not return to the game. A match is not considered valid if there are fewer than 7 players on either team.

Commentary: The selection and role of substitutes is an important consideration for the coach. The game situation itself will indicate when substitution is required, and the coach should be ready to make the decision. In youth games the number of allowed substitutions is higher than the number permitted by the international body, in order to give more players time to participate. The coach should be ready with at least 1 substitute for each of the following positions: goalkeeper, forward, fullback, attacking midfielder, and defensive midfielder.

LAW IV. PLAYERS' EQUIPMENT

A player shall not wear anything that is dangerous to another player. Bars of leather or rubber may be worn across the soles of the shoes as long as they are at least 1/2 inch wide. Studs are permitted on the soles of the shoes, but they must be rounded, at least 1/2 inch in diameter, and not more than 3/4 inch long. Studs molded as part of the sole must be of soft material and, if there are at least 10 on a sole, have a minimum diameter of 3/8 inch. The goalkeeper must wear colors that distinguish him from the other players and the referee.

Commentary: Shoes should be selected according to the surface of the field and its condition. On soft fields long studs are preferred; in fact, the softer the field, the longer the studs should be. Shoes with studs molded into the soles are preferred for harder fields. For artificial surfaces, sneakers should be considered. Shin guards should be worn by all players. Shirt material depends on climatic conditions; in hot, humid weather short-sleeved perforated shirts are recommended.

LAW V. REFEREES

The referee is in complete charge of the game. He is the timekeeper and keeps a record of the contest. The referee is empowered to stop play for injury or other reasons and to restart it when ready. He also may end the game due to inclement weather, spectator interference, etc. The referee administers penalties and cautions or expels players for misconduct. His decisions are final.

Commentary: Courteous behavior toward the referee brings better results than confrontation. Antagonism breeds antagonism, and an amiable manner is usually returned. Furthermore, a player who disputes the referee's decision incurs a penalty.

LAW VI. LINESMEN

There are 2 linesmen. Their chief duty is to indicate when the ball is out of play and which side is entitled to the corner kick, goal kick, or throw-in. The linesmen are equipped with flags, which they use to signal to the referee. By signaling, they assist him in controlling the game.

Commentary: The linesmen are an extension of the referee and should be treated as such. The coach can use them to communicate with the referee when, for instance, he wishes to make a substitution.

LAW VII. DURATION OF THE GAME

Soccer is played in 2 periods of 45 minutes each. Time lost due to injury or other causes is added on to the playing times at the discretion of the referee. Time is extended at the end of a period, if necessary, to allow for a penalty kick. The halftime interval shall not exceed 5 minutes, except by consent of the referee.

Commentary: The coach must prepare the team to perform at top efficiency during the entire game. The psychological, physical, and tactical intensity during the last minute of play should be equal to that of the first minute of play. However, the team should be coached to adjust its tactics as time is running out. For example, if it is winning and there are only 10 minutes left in the game, maintaining possession of the ball should be the team's objective. If it is losing, more fullbacks should be sent into the attack.

LAW VIII. THE START OF PLAY

A kickoff is used to start play at the beginning of the game, after a goal has been scored, and after halftime. The ball is placed on the center spot, and the kicker must send it into the opponent's half of the field. All other players must remain in their half of the field, and no opposing player may be within the center circle (that is, within 10 yards of the ball). The ball is in play after it has traveled the distance of its own circumference. The kicker may not play the ball again until it has been touched by another player.

The toss of a coin determines which team gets to decide whether to kick off first or to have its choice of ends at the beginning of the game. After a team scores a goal, the other team kicks off. Following halftime, ends are changed and the kickoff is made by the team that did not kick off to start the game.

When restarting play from causes other than those just mentioned or those mentioned elsewhere in the laws, and providing the ball has not passed over the touchline or goal line, the referee drops the ball at the place where it was when play was suspended, and it is in play when it touches the ground.

Commentary: The coach must determine whether it is to his team's advantage to gain the choice of ends or possession of the ball at the start of play. The condition of the field, the direction and intensity of the wind, and the position of the sun are some of the factors that should influence the choice of ends. Usually, the advantageous end is chosen at the start of a game in hopes that the team will be able to take an early lead. Besides, conditions may change in the second half of the game. The team should have set plays for kickoffs, drop balls, and other restart situations.

LAW IX. BALL IN AND OUT OF PLAY

The ball is out of play when it has wholly crossed the goal line or touchline, whether on the ground or in the air, and when the game has been stopped by the referee. The ball is in play at all other times, including when it rebounds from the goalposts and off officials who are on the field of play.

Commentary: Too often players stop when only a part of the ball has crossed a boundary line. Remember: the entire ball must cross the line before play is halted.

LAW X. METHOD OF SCORING

A goal is scored when the whole of the ball has passed over the goal line, between the goalposts and under the crossbar, providing it has not been thrown, carried, or propelled by hand or arm by a player of the attacking side. The team scoring most goals wins. If no goals are scored or if an equal number of goals are scored by each team, the game is declared a draw.

Commentary: Scoring goals is the essence of soccer. Any method can be used to shoot provided it is not specifically prohibited by the laws.

LAW XI. OFFSIDE

A player is offside if he is nearer his opponent's goal line than the ball at the moment the ball is played unless: he is in his own half of the field; 2 opponents (the goalkeeper counts) are nearer their own goal line than he is; the ball last touched an opponent or was last played by him; or he received the ball directly from a goal kick, corner kick, throw-in, or drop ball. The penalty for being offisde is an indirect free kick by a player of the opposing team from the place where the infringement occurred. Even though a player may be technically offside, the penalty is not called unless, in the opinion of the referee, he is interfering with play or with an opponent or is seeking to gain an advantage by being offside.

Commentary: On attack, players should always be aware of their position as it relates to the offside rule. Defensively, the offside trap—luring an attacker into an offside position—can be used to tremendous advantage. If the attacker is declared offside, the defensive team will not only gain possession of the ball but will also disrupt the rhythm of their opponents. The defensive team should be ready with backup plays in the event that the referee does not call the offside.

LAW XII. FOULS AND MISCONDUCT

A player who intentionally commits any of the following offenses shall be penalized by awarding a direct free kick to the opposing side from the place where the offense occurred: kicking or attempting to kick an opponent; tripping an opponent; jumping at an opponent; charging an opponent in a violent or dangerous manner; or charging from behind unless the opponent is obstructing; striking or attempting to strike an opponent; holding or pushing an opponent; and carrying, striking, or propelling the ball with the hands or arms (except for the goalkeeper within his own penalty area).

Should a defending player intentionally commit one of these

offenses within the penalty area, a penalty kick is awarded the opposing team.

A player commiting any of the following offenses shall be penalized by awarding an indirect free kick to the opposing side from the place where the offense occurred: playing in a dangerous manner; charging fairly when the ball is not within playing distance of the players concerned and they are not trying to play it; when not playing the ball, intentionally obstructing an opponent; charging the goalkeeper except when he is holding the ball, obstructing an opponent, or has moved outside his goal area; and when playing as goalkeeper, indulging in tactics designed to delay the game to his team's advantage.

A player is cautioned if he enters, reenters, or leaves the field without the referee's permission; persistently infringes the laws; shows by word or action dissent from a decision made by the referee; or is guilty of ungentlemanly conduct. An indirect free kick results from the last three cautions and, at the referee's discretion, may result from the first.

A player is sent off the field if he is guilty of violent conduct or serious foul play; uses foul or abusive language; or persists in misconduct after receiving a caution. If play is stopped when a player is ordered off the field, the game is resumed by an indirect free kick awarded to the opposing side from the place where the infringement occurred.

Commentary: Every player should know the offenses that result in direct and indirect free kicks. This awareness can be instilled in one-on-one training.

LAW XIII. FREE KICK

There are two types of free kicks: *direct* (from which a goal can be scored) and *indirect* (from which a goal cannot be scored unless the ball has been played or touched by a player other than the kicker before it passes through the goal). When a player is taking a free kick inside his own penalty area, all opposing players must remain outside the area and at least 10 yards from the ball. When he is taking a free kick outside his own penalty area, all opposing players must be at least 10 yards from the ball unless they are standing on their own goal line between the goalposts. On free kicks the ball is in play once it has traveled the distance of its own circumference, and the ball cannot be played again by the kicker until it has been touched by another player.

Commentary: As with other still-ball situations, the attacking team has a better chance of scoring on a free kick if they have set plays, or predetermined moves, to follow up the kick. Set plays require correct timing, proper execution, and deception. On direct free kicks, players with the ability to bend, or curve, balls around an opposing wall of defenders are especially useful. On defense, the organization of the wall should take place quickly and without the assistance of the goalkeeper.

LAW XIV. PENALTY KICK

If a defending player is within his own team's penalty area when he intentionally commits any one of the nine offenses that result in the awarding of a direct free kick (see Law XII), the opposing team is granted a penalty kick. The penalty kick is taken from the penalty spot, and all players (except the defending goalkeeper) must stay outside of the penalty area and at least 10 yards away from the ball. The defending goalkeeper must remain stationary on his goal line between the goalposts until the kick is taken. The person making the kick must propel the ball forward and cannot play the ball a second time until it has been touched by another player.

Commentary: Players on the attacking team should position themselves around the penalty area in anticipation of the ball rebounding off the goalkeeper, the goalposts, or the crossbar. Players should be given experience in making penalty kicks, and the shooter must be prepared for the psychological pressure that accompanies this situation.

LAW XV. THROW-IN

To restart play after the whole of the ball has passed over a touch-line, the ball is thrown in from the point where it crossed the line by a player of the team opposing that of the person who last touched the ball. The thrower must use both hands and deliver the ball from over his head, while keeping part of each foot either on or outside the touchline. He cannot again play the ball until it has been touched by another player. A goal may not be scored directly from a throw-in. Opposing players are not allowed to dance about or try to impede the thrower.

Commentary: Because the offside law is not in effect during throw-ins, they can be an effective attacking weapon. Individuals capable of making long throws are especially valuable on a team. Set plays should be designed according to the location of the throw-ins and the abilities of the players.

LAW XVI. GOAL KICK

When the whole of the ball passes over the goal line (excluding that portion of the line between the goalposts) and it was last played by a member of the attacking team, it is kicked into play by a member of the defending team from a point within that half of the goal area nearest to where it crossed the goal line. The ball must be kicked beyond the penalty area, and players of the opposing team must remain outside that area while the kick is being taken. The kicker cannot play the ball a second time until it has been touched by another player, and a goal may not be scored directly from a goal kick.

Commentary: Although any member of the defending team may take the goal kick, the goalkeeper usually performs this duty in order to maintain the numerical balance of players downfield. The main objective of the person making the goal kick is to enable his team to retain possession of the ball. Thus long, high kicks downfield are not in order. It is safer for the kicker to play the ball short, allowing time for his team to build up the attack.

LAW XVII. CORNER KICK

When the whole of the ball passes over the goal line (excluding that portion of the line between the goalposts) and it was last played by a member of the defending team, the attacking team is allowed a corner kick. The ball is kicked from the quarter circle (corner area) at the nearest corner flag post, which must not be moved. A goal may be scored directly from a corner kick. Opposing players must remain at least 10 yards from the ball until it is in play, or has traveled the distance of its own circumference. The kicker may not play the ball a second time until it has been touched by another player.

Commentary: Set plays should be developed to capitalize on corner-kick situations. Tha ball can be kicked to a teammate or propelled directly into the goal area. Players should practice bending, or curving, the ball around the defenders and kicking at varying speeds and heights. Since the offside law is not in effect during corner kicks, the players' runs are not restricted.

FIELD DIMENSIONS AND TERMINOLOGY

As already mentioned, you must be sure of the specific rules of your league. You must also carefully check the size of the playing field. It really does make a difference when youngsters practice on one size field, only to play their games on another. Many leagues HAVE to adapt their fields, because they're just smaller.

The field in the following diagram is regulation size. We suggest you diagram your own field so that when you work on your practice plans you can be sure you have enough room and that your drills are run on the same size field as the one you play your games on.

The old rope trick. In most cases, your practices will be conducted on fields without lines, corners, and sometimes even without goals. But, your practice dimensions *must* match game field dimensions. It does no good to work on penalty kicks if, because your field has no penalty spot, you merely guess and end up kicking from 10 yards.

How do you make sure your cones for goals are exactly 8 yards apart? Take a piece of string or rope at least as long as the width of your field (regulation, 50 yards) and *tie knots at the distances you will need for your field*—for example, 6 yards, 8 yards, 10 yards, 12 yards, 18 yards. This way, when you decide to run a drill from 10 yards out, *you know exactly how far ten yards is!* This simple trick is a helpful tool for coaches and coaching.

FIELD DIMENSIONS & TERMINOLOGY

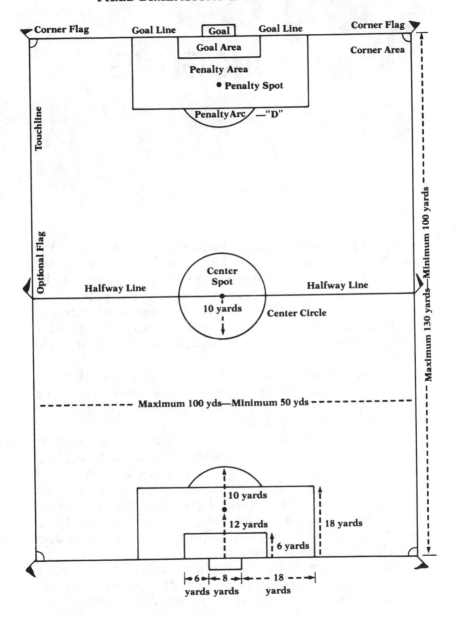

6

JUGGLING

Jugglers keep balls, hoops, clubs, and other objects in the air by using mainly their hands and arms. In soccer, however, the player keeps the soccer ball in the air by using all parts of his body *except* his arms and hands.

Aside from helping a player become more familiar with the ball, juggling may be the best way to improve a soccer player's balance in a short period of time. It's also fun!

Be certain to emphasize to your players that they are not just juggling to put on a show. It's intended to improve their touch and balance, timing, and foot-eye, thigh-eye and forehead-eye coordination.

Juggling with the *foot* forces players to use the same concentration they would when shooting the ball. Juggling with the *thigh* forces them to concentrate as they would when receiving an air ball with the thigh. Juggling with the *head* uses the same forehead-eye coordination a player uses when heading a ball for a shot or pass. Juggling, then, is a purposeful skill that will improve touch, balance, and eye coordination with the ball.

Start off by giving each player a ball; if that isn't possible, have partners share a ball. Be certain that players are spread out to avoid collisions. With younger kids you'll want to *really* spread out to prevent a roller derby situation.

1. Thigh. Have the player toss the ball into the air and, as the ball comes down, bring his thigh up and hit the ball up in the air again; the player should catch the ball with his hands and bring the juggling leg back down to the ground.

Remind your players that the thigh should be parallel to the ground or the ball will bounce forward or into the player's body, that they should hit the ball with the center of their thigh, and that the juggling leg should return to the ground after each juggle.

After the ball has been juggled once and caught, the player should try to juggle two consecutive times and catch it. If he is successful with two, let him try to juggle three times. Once the players are able to juggle three times in a row, turn 'em loose and see how many times they can juggle before missing.

2. The instep (the part of the foot where the shoelaces are). Using the same progression as with the thigh, have the players toss and juggle the ball once, twice, and three times, before turning them loose. When juggling with the instep, the toe must be pointed and the ankle locked; this simulates the position of the foot when shooting. The laces should be parallel to the ground when contact is made, and the ball should not have any spin on it.

3. Head: Follow the same juggling procedure as established above. Instruct the players to hit the ball on the forehead with their eyes open. They hit the ball, the ball doesn't hit them. Have them lean their heads back to get the back of the head parallel to the ground. They will have to bend their knees a bit as well. The heading force will come from the neck, back, and legs as they juggle.

JUGGLING GAMES

Once the basic juggling techniques have been taught, all sorts of *challenges* are possible. Players can start juggling with the thigh and save the ball with their foot before it hits the ground; players can start with their head and save only with the foot; or alternate body parts by juggling with the head, thigh, foot, in sequence. The team can have fun seeing which player can juggle the ball farthest across the field, total distance determined by where he last touched the ball. (This precludes just kicking the ball across the field.) Another contest is to see how many times a player can turn in a circle while juggling. Be creative!

PARTNER JUGGLING

There are a number of partner juggling exercises as well. Have two partners stand about four to five yards away from each other. One partner begins juggling and after three to five juggles, must juggle the ball over to his partner. His players juggles three to five times and then juggles the ball back. This exercise can also involve three players. Keep in mind our philosophy of not asking kids to do things they can't do. Some youngsters find it difficult to juggle, so don't force them. Instead, allow players to juggle after a bounce. This will give them more time to get ready for each touch. If this proves to be too difficult, bring out some beach balls or balloons for the activity. Besides helping them to improve, it can be lots of fun.

Goalkeepers can also have fun juggling using all parts of their body. They can challenge each other by punching a soccer ball in the air with one hand or with two hands together. They can also hand juggle while running across the field or with a partner.

So, have your players juggle in practice and encourage them to practice at home on their own. The only investment your players make is their time, which is a small price to pay, considering the improvement they will exhibit in touch-the-ball and body coordination.

7

THE SKILLS OF SOCCER

There are some skills that *all* soccer players must have to be successful. Without them, the game is reduced to some-one kicking the ball down the field and someone else running after it. Unfortunately, many games are played in this manner and kickball would more realistically de-scribe what is taking place. It is up to the coaches to demand that youngsters not just kick the ball, but rather exhibit the ability to *control the ball* and then do something constructive with it. The player must feel that the ball is a part of him and not an alien being trying to trip him up. Only through *perfect* repetition of the skills can a skillful player emerge.

SHOOTING

If there is one weakness Americans display most in inter-national soccer, it is the inability to put the ball into the net. One reason is that youngsters don't spend enough time actually shooting the ball as they would in a game. A coach may simply place a ball down on the ground in front of the goal and have the players run up and kick it. We're not helping our youngsters become proficient shooters or scorers with this type of practice.

While this type of fundamental exercise with a still ball is important for younger players, they will have to progress to shooting moving balls, balls that come at them from different angles, balls that are on the ground, and balls that come to them in the air. Let's look at some of the basic elements and "rules" of shooting:

1. **Regardless of where you strike the ball, your ankle must be locked.** Remind your players to keep their head down and their toe down. In keeping the head down, they will concentrate on striking the center of the ball; keeping their toe down will present the proper surface to the ball.

2. **It doesn't matter how hard you swing your leg, if you only hit part of the ball, it won't go far.** Players must strike the center of the ball if they want to drive the ball hard.

3. **When striking the ball, your players must have the knee of the kicking foot even with the ball.** If the knee is behind the ball when kicked, it will cause the player to have to reach for it, and thus strike it below the midline— causing the ball to fly up.

4. **The non-kicking foot must step in the direction you want the shot to go.** If you watch carefully, you will see that your players' accuracy will be in direct correlation with this simple rule.

5. **The size of the feet can create difficulty when trying to get players to kick the ball with their instep.** Hate to say it, Coach, but some kids have bigger feet than others, and the bigger-footed kids will have some problems kicking with the instep.

Let's examine this foot problem a little more closely: players with bigger feet have difficulty because they are sometimes afraid of stubbing their toe on the ground, and so will raise their leg a bit and only strike the ball with the *bottom third of the foot.*

Big-footed players also tend to bring their toe up and curl their foot around the ball as they kick. This generates little power because the ankle unlocks.

How to help the big-footed player strike the ball with the instep: (Get a bigger ball! No, only kidding. . . .)

Players with bigger feet should approach the ball from a 45-degree angle and step farther away from the ball. Then, by turning their big toe outward and striking the ball with the inside eyelets of their shoe, they will gain the same result.

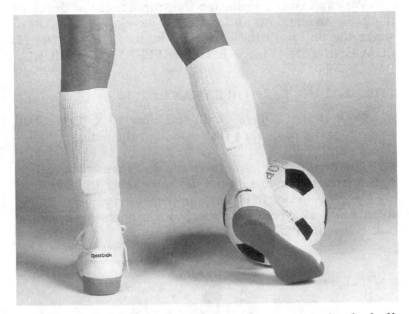

You can also direct big-footed players to strike the ball with the toe DOWN and inward, using the outside eyelets of the shoe.

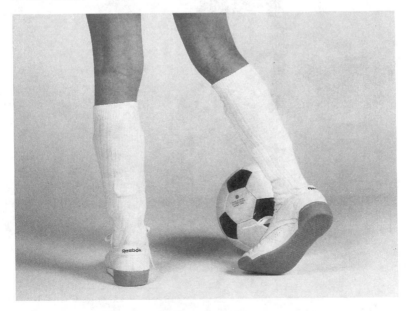

We can't over emphasize the importance of developing *power* in our shots and passes by developing the skill to strike the ball with the instep of the foot. WORK ON IT, COACH, AND YOU'LL SEE THE DIFFERENCE QUICKLY.

THE BENDING BALL OR BANANA KICK

Now that we have explained how to kick the ball straight and strong, let's take a look at the bending ball— the banana kick.

The bending or banana kick results when the ball is struck by your players *across the ball*, rather than straight on. Needless to say, in order to make it curve, it must be in the air and as a result we teach our players to strike the ball *below the midline of the ball*.

When trying to bend the ball around defenders, a defensive wall, or the goalie's outstretched hands, the banana ball is used.

Remember, the ball is struck with the inside of the shoe above the big toe and the inside eyelets, across the ball and under its midline.

HEADING

We use our feet to propel the ball, and our thighs or foot to stop the ball, but the toughest trick for your players is using the head to either propel the ball or gather it. Kids just aren't used to hitting their heads against a moving object. But anyone who knows soccer realizes that heading is one of the most important skills in the game. Let's look at the progression for teaching heading:

1. Your players' attitude must be that *they are going to hit the ball, rather than let the ball hit them.*

2. Your players must be taught that the proper place to make contact with the ball in a header is with the forehead, not the top of the head.

3. The only way your players can ensure making contact with the forehead is for them to *keep their eyes open,* the most important skill for heading.

4. Your players should clench their teeth, which tightens their neck muscles and so firms the position of the head; this results in a more powerful header. (It also prevents biting the tongue.)

5. To increase power, your players should *arch their backs.*

6. A sharp bending forward after contact also results in increased power, so your players must understand that heading is learned from the *waist up.*

> **Reminder:** STRIKE THE BALL WITH THE CENTER OF
> THE FOREHEAD. KEEP THE EYES OPEN. HIT THE
> BALL—DON'T LET THE BALL HIT YOU.

PASSING

There's a saying in soccer that if you can't pass, you can't
play soccer. That statement is true. There is nothing more
frustrating to a soccer team than having a player standing
in front of the goal, wide open, ready to score a winning
goal, only to have the passer not reach him or miss him
with the ball.

> **The Rules:** YOUR PLAYERS MUST BE ABLE TO PASS
> THE BALL TO A MAN, OR TO A SPACE—AND WITH
> PROPER PACE.

Let's see what this means:

PROPER PACE . . .

Proper pace means that the ball is passed in such a
way that the receiver may ONE TOUCH the ball. He/she
may pass or shoot the ball without gathering it in and
stopping it, kicking it on immediately. But a ball that is
passed too softly (hospital ball) could hurt your teammate
(collision may result because the defender can get there
just as quickly as your teammate) and usually result in
loss of possession too. A ball struck too hard (the bullet)
usually results in the teammate not being able to gather
the ball. Needless to say, one-touching the bullet is almost
an impossibility. TWO TOUCHES, which means just what
it says—touching the ball twice (gather, kick)—is frankly
how most players play a pass. Of course, it must be
practiced. We'll deal with receiving later on.

TO A SPACE

The game of soccer is a game of space—space between people, space between the goalie and the goal posts, space between defender and attacker. Your passing players must often be looking to pass the ball into an AREA rather than directly to a man. This is passing into space. (The corresponding skill for the receiver is RUNNING INTO SPACE.) Remember, the receiver knows what space he/she is going to run into, the defender doesn't. This is one of the advantages to having possession of the ball: your passer must understand space, practice passing into it, and realize how important it is.

OTHER PASSING RULES

1. The foot doesn't lie. Whatever direction the foot is facing is the direction the ball will go.
2. Receivers can do more harm than good by yelling for the ball.

How often do your hear players yell for the ball, have it passed to them, only to see it lost? The fact is that if the offensive player hears the yell, so does the defensive player. Your players must pass ONLY WHEN THEY ARE READY.

PASSING SKILLS

Now let's look at the different types of passes and how to teach them.

PUSH PASS—The most frequently used pass in the game today is the push pass. The rules for teaching and practicing this pass are:

1. The ankle must be locked.
2. The kicking foot is turned sideways to the ball.

3. The ball is struck below the ankle bone and closer to the middle of the foot.

4. The ball is struck as close to the midline as possible.

5. After striking the ball, the player should raise his/ her knee up which will give the ball top spin, resulting in the ball moving more quickly.

6. The lower leg should swing through like a pendulum.

7. The non-kicking foot is pointed where? That's right, in the direction the player wants the ball to go.

If you ask your players to FREEZE after kicking the ball, you will be able to see if their technique is correct or not. If correct, the inside of the foot will be facing the receiver.

OUTSIDE OF THE FOOT PASS—The outside of the foot is often used for passing and the rules for using it are somewhat more difficult to teach, but nevertheless important:

1. When kicking the ball with the outside of the foot, the ANKLE MUST BE LOCKED. (Have you heard this enough?)

2. The player should point his/her toe DOWN, and inward.

3. The non-kicking foot should be turned slightly AWAY FROM THE BALL. That's different, eh? By stepping away, it will give the player a bit more room for the kicking foot to come through.

4. The heel of the kicking foot, when brought back to strike the ball, should be brought back BEHIND THE KNEE OF THE NON—KICKING FOOT.

5. Of course, we have our players strike the center of the ball, but this time with the "Little Piggy toe."

CHIP PASS—When the ball is lofted with backspin, it's called a chip. Here are the steps in teaching it:

1. The ball is struck with the INSIDE EYELETS of the shoe.

2. When bringing the kicking foot back, bring it back to the BACKSIDE.

3. The knee must SNAP when coming forward. Again, the best way to see if the technique is correct is to FREEZE the player after contact. Remember, the backspin will result only if the ball is struck below the midline with a LOCKED ANKLE.

RECEIVING

Now that you've taught your kids how to pass it and head it, let's deal with the guy on the other end—the RECEIVER.

In the past, receiving has been called trapping, though it doesn't matter what it is called. The skill demands mastering the art of gathering in the ball in order to do something else with it. Stress that RECEIVING ALWAYS LEADS TO SOMETHING ELSE; in that way your players are motivated to learn and work on this important skill. Simply put, when receiving the ball, the player will redirect the ball and either dribble, pass, or take a shot.

Here's how to teach receiving:

1. Players must be able to receive the ball with every legal body part—foot, thigh, head, chest, etc.

2. Players must "read" the flight or run of the ball so that he/she can center the body on the ball.

3. Once the ball flight or run is read, the player can decide which body part will receive the ball.

4. Next, your player is to PRESENT that body part to the ball.

5. As the ball makes contact, the body part must be DRAWN BACK slightly for the "give" that results in control.

6. A short HOP just before contact will help your players stay on their toes and off their heels, thus cushioning the blow and helping with control.

RECEIVING WITH DIFFERENT BODY PARTS

SOLE OF THE FOOT—It's easiest to teach players to receive with the bottom of the foot. Simply put, have each player lift their toe off the ground slightly as the ball is kicked their way, and cushion the ball as it makes contact.

Have your players pretend the ball is an egg and they will understand how lightly it must be touched.

SIDE OF THE FOOT (BALL IN THE AIR)—As the ball comes toward the player, he/she should angle the lower leg from the knee down to the foot. Then, using the inside of the foot and angling the leg over the ball, redirect it to the side of the foot and gather it.

This technique can be accomplished with either the inside or the outside of the ankle.

SIDE OF THE FOOT (BALL ON THE GROUND)—As the ball comes toward the player, he/she should bring the toe up and angle the foot to the side. Contact the ball with the side of the foot and redirect it.

BOTTOM THIRD OF THE FOOT OR LOWER INSTEP—This method is usually used for air balls. Have your players relax their ankle to cushion the ball. Then, by giving way a little, the player can literally catch the ball with the bottom third of the foot.

THIGH—The thigh is larger and softer than the other parts of the body, but the rules are the same: read the flight of the ball; present the surface (thigh); take a slight hop before contact; bring the leg down upon contact. Again, this obviously works only for air balls.

CHEST—For the chest "trap" it is important that you teach your players to make contact with HALF of the chest, rather than straight on. This is because with the sternum, or chest bone, right in the middle, balls taken straight on can bounce away. (A football receiver who has a perfectly thrown pass bounce off his chest because he let it go through his hands directly onto his shoulder pads illustrates the same principle.) Using half of the chest will result in contact with the fleshy part and provide more control. Also, the ball can be redirected easier. The rules for receiving with the chest, however, are the same as with other body parts.

HEAD—This may come as a surprise, but the head can also be used to receive the ball. How? Teach your players to "give" with the neck and back at contact and try to contact the ball as it is coming down. Obviously this means they will jump in the air to receive with the head.

Needless to say, your players should be taught to receive the ball with the foot whenever possible because any other reception requires TWO TOUCHES to control the ball and do something else with it.

DRIBBLING

Simply defined, dribbling consists of tiny touches of the ball, usually in close quarters. When dribbling, as in the performance of other skills of the game, players must be able to use all parts of the foot—the inside, outside, top, and sole. Your players must be able to change speed, change direction, and dribble with their heads up. (There are only two times when soccer players should have their heads down: when the player first touches the ball, and when it is last touched.) Keeping the head up is essential because otherwise your players will not be able to see their teammates, defenders, or the goal.

CHANGING SPEED—Successful control of the ball while dribbling means that your players must be able to alter their pace of dribbling. A defending player has a much better chance of taking the ball away if the dribbler continues at an even pace. Teach your players to vary their speed and they will have much more success keeping the ball away.

CHANGING DIRECTION—If your players can change speed, but only in a straight line, they aren't going to be very difficult to stop. Players must be able to move the ball back and forth and change position while dribbling. Starting right and going left; starting left and going right; even starting forward and sometimes moving back are direction changes that must be taught and practiced.

HEAD UP—Just to reiterate, your players can't play if they can't see. The head-up principle must be stressed and restressed. If you can't *see,* you can't be successful in soccer.

ONE FOOT VERSUS TWO FEET—Many coaches of soccer emphasize that a player must be able to play with both feet. This is certainly true, but coaches often overemphasize this skill.

When talking about and teaching dribbling, few players are equally proficient with either foot. Most of them have a dominant foot and an efficient foot. (Franz Beckenbauer, an outstanding German player who played with Cosmos in the United States, played few balls with his left foot because his right foot was so dominant he could do anything with it. By using both the inside and outside of his right foot he became one of the greatest passers in soccer history.)

The fact is, players can attack much more quickly while dribbling with only one foot.

DRIVING

Driving means that instead of working in a small area with many defenders, the player has more room and can literally pass the ball to himself. The best way to describe driving is by example: Perhaps your wing is turning at midfield and has beaten the defender. He doesn't want the ball to slow him down. His best bet, then, is to push the ball ahead of him into space so that as he runs toward the ball, he can make a decision on what to do next. Just how far he pushes it will depend on how much space he has to work with.

SHIELDING

All good dribblers must know shielding. Similar to the basketball technique where the dribbler keeps the ball away from the defender with his body, shielding in soccer means that the dribbler keeps his body between the defender and the ball. Don't allow players to turn their backs on the defender, which invites an easy reach for the ball, either through or around the dribbler's legs. When the dribbler turns his back he will also have trouble beating the defender one on one—he can't see the defender or his teammates.

Proper shielding technique is a sideways turn—which makes the player WIDER and shields the ball more effectively. This also allows your player to lean into the defender and open up his field of vision to better see a teammate or take a shot on goal.

WRONG

RIGHT

THROW-INS

When the ball passes the sideline or touchline, the team that didn't knock it out executes the throw-in. Here are the rules for teaching the throw-in:

1. The thrower must hold the ball and throw it with two hands.

2. The ball must start from behind the head and be released over the head.

3. Both feet must remain on the ground during the throw. Throw-ins must be practiced in order to prevent illegal motion which results in the other team getting the ball.

4. The body must face in the direction of the throw.

5. The ball cannot be thrown into the goal. It must touch someone else first, including the goalkeeper!

8
EXERCISES TO IMPROVE SKILLS (Techniques)

It is the nature of the game that all of the players on the field must be able to perform all of the sport's various skills. Each player, regardless of position, will be called upon to head, pass, receive, shoot, and dribble during the game.

Your job, as a youth league coach, is to teach these skills and drill your players on when and how to use them.

At higher levels of play, players assigned to certain positions for the majority of a game may spend practice time doing *functional* training. This involves backs, midfielders, and strikers (forwards), training to do (technically and tactically) what they will be called upon to do in a game, *most* of the time. As you may have noticed, this book is geared toward an overall development of skill for all players.

Many of the exercises introduced here involve using more than one skill at a time. As a coach you must determine which single skill you are trying to improve upon during an offensive tactic and *comment only on that skill, even if you are inclined to comment on others.* During play, try to determine if this exercise is meeting your goal to improve a specific skill. If it isn't, try to break down the exercise to a more fundamental level.

For example, if shooting was the goal of an exercise, but you did not get very many shots on goal, then change the exercise. Replace the defender with a cone (or a coach playing passive defense) and explain that a shot must be taken every time; or that the defender is not allowed to steal the ball. Don't be afraid to change the exercise if you have given it a fair chance to succeed at meeting a particular goal and it hasn't worked. We can't stress enough the importance of being flexible and understanding with your little people. If a drill you are using doesn't work, for goodness sakes END IT and move on. A skill practiced incorrectly will result in that skill being done incorrectly at game time.

THINGS TO THINK ABOUT WHEN DESIGNING DRILLS

1. *If you ask a player to do something he can't do, you are wrong; if you ask a player to do something he can do and he doesn't, then he's wrong.* If you decide he can do it and he doesn't, then you, as coach, must try to determine why he can't. Is it his subtle misunderstanding of what to do? Is he able to perform the skill but only under limited pressure? Can he do what you ask, but only three times out of ten? When you determine the reason he is unsuccessful, then you must develop a program for him to be successful—or accept the fact that at *this time* he is not able to perform that skill.

2. *Youngsters will remember about 50 percent of what they are told, 60 percent of what they see, 75 percent of what they do, and 85 percent of what they teach.* Quite often coaches find themselves pressured with limited practice time and will only *tell* a youngster what to do. Some may show what they want as well. The most successful coaches will give their players sufficient opportunities to try the task and some may even ask their players to explain what they are doing as a coach would. In this way the player learns, without question, what is expected.

3. *When teaching a technique, it must be done perfectly.* Even the most inexperienced coach can demonstrate a skill efficiently if it is done in slow motion, step by step. Players must see and then practice the technique perfectly. The old adage, "practice makes perfect," is wrong. *Practice makes permanent; perfect practice makes perfect.*

4. *When coaching, stay positive and stay clear of using the word "don't."* Instead, instruct your players to *do* something. By using a positive statement, you reinforce your instructions in their mind. (The same can be said for negative statements. If someone were to say to you, "Don't think of a pink elephant," you would immediately think of a pink elephant!) If you want your players to think of certain things on the field, reinforce them positively. "Tommy, pass the ball more" will help Tommy more than "Don't dribble so much, Tommy."

5. *Avoid "waste" drills that take up valuable time.* Use exercises that develop what players will do in a game. Each exercise should have a purpose and help you meet team goals. Remember that when setting up a practice area (grid), the size of the area will depend upon the number of players and their skill level. Don't be afraid to adjust the size of the grid if you have miscalculated.

6. *Distance rule.* As we said in Rule 1: If you ask a player to do something he can't do, you are wrong. Similarly, if you should ask him to do something he can do, but you make the conditions such that he can't, you're wrong again. For example, if you are working on receiving and your players cannot pass accurately from more than 10 yards away, they will surely fail if they are placed 25 yards apart.

Here are some exercises to help turn your young ones into America's first Pelés. Keep in mind that many of the exercises use a number of skills. Stress only the skills you are trying to improve.

SHOOTING

Remember the rules: HEAD DOWN/TOE DOWN/LOCK
THE ANKLE AND DON'T LET IT MOVE; STRIKE THE
CENTER OF THE BALL WITH THE LACES.

---

1. Tap/tap. Many youngsters don't know what it feels
like to have the ball hit their instep (laces). So let them
kneel on one knee and bang a ball on the laces of their front
foot.

With that accomplished, have a coach place his foot just above the midline of the ball and let each player strike the center of the ball with their laces solidly. Make certain they don't swing too hard and miss or the coach may need new shins.

2. Punting. With that in mind, now let the players get a partner and share one ball. From a 10-yard distance have both players punt the ball back and forth to one another like a football. They should concentrate on striking the ball just before it hits the ground. Explain that the ball is not allowed to travel higher than their waist. Tell them that you want to see how many times in a row they can catch the ball. This exercise will help remove the fear some youngsters have of hitting their toe on the ground as they shoot.

3. Still balls. After reviewing the proper technique of shooting the ball, both partners now shoot still balls on the ground to one another from 10 yards away. Tell the players to pretend that their shot is just a pass (around the goalkeeper) and to strike the ball solidly but not so hard that their partner can't control the ball. At this point, some players may still be afraid of stubbing their toe and make the two most common mistakes: raising their foot at contact and curling their toes up and around the ball (unlock the ankle).

It may be necessary to go back to a few of the previous exercises to try and correct these problems.

4. Moving balls. Have the players back up to about 20 yards and remain with a partner. Now the player with the ball will push the ball forward 2–3 yards, run toward it, step and shoot. Immediately you will find many youngsters shooting balls over the goal height of 8 feet. Explain that this happens because, as they step even with the ball to shoot, the ball continues to roll and lies ahead of their foot when they actually hit it. So they reach for the ball and strike under its middle, sending it flying into the air. The solution is to step *beyond* the ball when kicking a moving ball. How far the player steps beyond the ball depends on how fast it is rolling. Have the player continue to push the balls ahead and strike them. You should see improvement.

5. Slalom and shoot. This exercise offers more of a gamelike situation. Set up four cones on each side of where the penalty area meets the penalty arc. (See Field Dimensions Diagram in Chapter 5.)

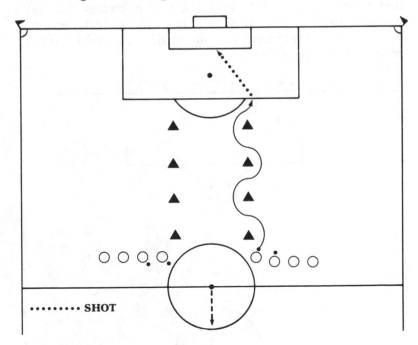

Have two groups of players line up behind these cones; the cones should be about 2 yards apart. The first person on line dribbles in and out of the cones (slalom) and shoots. As soon as the shooter strikes the ball, the first person in the other line begins. Be certain to stress that players should shoot with both feet and keep the shot low. After a few minutes of shooting, stop the action and remind the players of the importance of keeping the ball low: low shots are harder for a young goalkeeper to dive and save; low balls may deflect off a post or body and go in (even if it is a wide shot); low shots may be blocked by the goalkeeper and the rebound kicked in. A goalkeeper may be screened or "blinded" by his teammate on a low kick; a high shot will simply sail over the goal.

6. Coach's toss. The next shooting exercise is a more strenuous one-on-one (1-V-1) confrontation. Again, form two lines 6 yards outside each of the posts. The coach stands 25 yards away and says go. The first person in each line runs out to the D and the coach passes the ball between each of the players. Alternate air and ground passes. The players fight to control the ball and have five seconds to get off a shot.

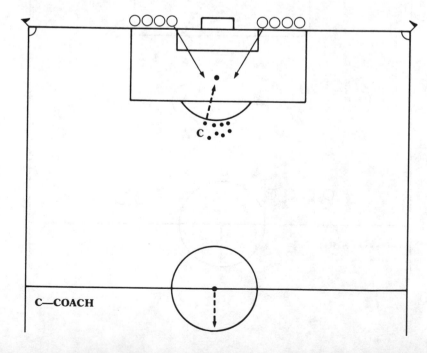

C—COACH

7. Eight-second shot drill. Set up a mini-field 35 yards long, at the regular field width. Put a goalie in each goal. Have the goalies round up a few back-up balls, ready to be put into play. Form teams of 4 to 6 players on a side. The object is for them to score goals *as a team*. There are only two restrictions: the goalie can only roll the ball out rather than kick or throw it, and as soon as a field player touches the ball, a shot must be taken on goal within 8 seconds. (Be flexible with the time.)

During each of these shooting exercises it is imperative to stress the proper mental approach toward shooting. Players must realize that they have a responsibility and obligation to shoot when the opportunity presents itself.

A missed opportunity can never be gotten back! Your players' attitude must be, "If I'm within range, I must shoot!"

HEADING

> **Remember the rules:** EYES OPEN; HIT THE FOREHEAD; TIGHTEN TEETH; HIT THE BALL, DON'T LET THE BALL HIT YOU.

Heading is one of the more difficult skills to teach youngsters because they tend to fear getting hit on their nose, cheek, mouth, eye, top of their head, etc. Remind them that in order to head the ball on the part that won't hurt (the forehead) they must keep their eyes open. That is easier said than done, however. To develop your young players' confidence in heading the ball, a wise investment might be a couple of nerf balls. Then they can miss painlessly as they teach themselves the skill.

1. Thanks, I needed that. Have your players pair up and share a ball with their partner. In turn, each partner holds the ball in both hands and hits his forehead 10 times. When finished, both players know what it feels like to have their head hit a ball in the correct place. They also realize that they are still in good shape and ready for another challenge.

2. Head to your partner. The first partner now attempts to hold the ball in both hands and head it out of his hands to his partner 5 yards away. Explain that to get the extra power for heading, it is necessary to arch the back and then snap forward.

3. Heading the tossed ball. This next step will build your players' confidence in heading a tossed ball. Young players may have difficulty tossing a soccer ball, so the coach should be ready to toss it for them. The age and skill of the players will determine if you want to use nerf or regular balls. For ten- or eleven-year-olds you might even think about gently tossing tennis balls underhand. It will help them to concentrate on the ball. They will also realize that anyone who can head a tennis ball, can't possibly miss a big soccer ball. Remember not to be farther than 10 yards when you toss.

4. Toss and move. (NOTE: These exercises require a good toss. You may have to be the tosser.) This exercise continues the tossing and heading drill while the players are moving. Partners should stand about 2–3 yards apart. The tosser runs backward across the field as the header runs forward. The partners toss and head back to one another as they go across the field. When they reach the other side, have the partners switch roles, the tosser running forward and the header running backward. This drill presumes a high level of skill; only you can determine if your players are up to it.

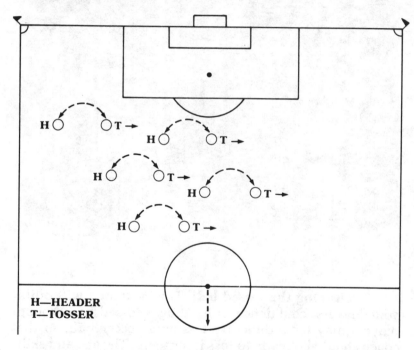

H—HEADER
T—TOSSER

5. Directing with the head. The next skill your soccer players need to develop is the ability to direct the ball with their head. Make certain that your players have lots of room. The tosser begins by making an underhand toss to the header. Immediately, the tosser moves to the right or left. The header must perceive the direction in which the tosser moves and head it to him.

6. Individual head juggling. Each player juggles the ball in the air using the head only.

Here's a fun idea. Have heading contests at practice using the drills just described and give awards for the leaders when the practice is finished. Lollipops may be an appropriate reward. Sugarless, of course!

7. Run-on header. These exercises are more game-related. The simplest is to have a coach stand at the side of the goal with the soccer balls. One player acts as a goalie while the others line up even with the opposite post about 18 yards away. The first header runs toward the center of the goal. Toss the ball in the air about 8 yards from the goal. The player times the flight of the ball and tries to head it in to the goal.

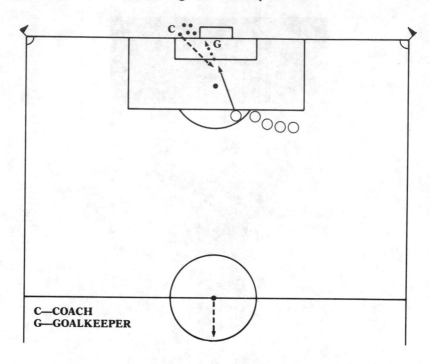

C—COACH
G—GOALKEEPER

Then the header becomes the new goalie. The previous goalie chases the ball, sets it down by the coach and moves to the end of the heading line. For a challenge, place cones approximately 12 yards in front of the goal. The header must now leap over the cones, regain his balance, find the ball, and head it in to the goal. The coach must time his toss to give the header a chance to head the ball. Allow more time for the less athletic youngster.

8. Lay-back shoot. The next exercise combines heading and a shot on goal by a second player. The heading player stands with his back to the goal. He is on the penalty spot (12 yards away). The remaining players line up with a ball at the edge of the penalty arc (D) and penalty area line. The first player in line tosses the ball to the header and moves to the D. The header lays the ball back to the tosser who shoots on goal. The shooter now

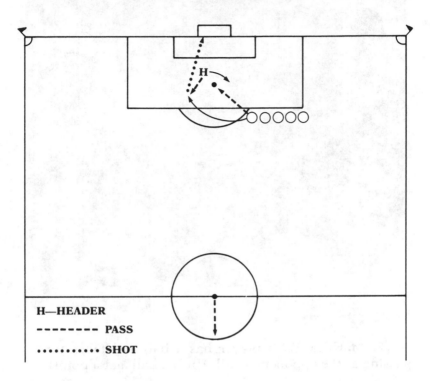

H—HEADER

-------- PASS

••••••••• SHOT

runs to the penalty spot and becomes the new header. The previous header rotates to the end of the line. Remember, the kid hits the ball, the ball doesn't hit the kid!

PASSING

Remember the rule: PASS TO A MAN OR SPACE WITH PROPER PACE.

1. **Wishbone soccer.** Have partners alternate standing with their legs as goals about 2 feet apart. Have each partner see how many times in five tries he can pass the ball through the other player's legs.

2. Marbles. Each player has a ball and takes turns passing at the opponent's ball. Hit the ball, get a point!

It's much harder to hit a moving target than a stationary one. It's also considerably harder to hit a moving target with a moving object! Now that your players have been drilled on the fundamental stage of the game, we must move on to the *match-related level.* Match-related means drills that closely approximate the *pressure* of a game.

3. The King drill. Start off by dividing the team into pairs with each pair sharing one ball. Make sure that you block off the goal area with cones and keep it *off limits* for safety. Now, on half of the field have the players with the ball begin to dribble in and around all of the other dribblers and defenders. (The dribblers are all dribbling in and out of one another and their partners.) The players without the ball are also moving all over the field, taking mental "pictures" of continually changing spaces created by the movement of players. The dribbler will not pass the ball until he is ready and only then will he pass to *his* partner. This means that he should make eye contact with his partner, indicating, "Here it comes." If he cannot do that, he shouldn't pass. The ball must be passed on the ground. The partner without the ball must not make a run for the ball into space until eye contact signals that his partner is ready to pass.

This exercise helps alleviate two of the most frustrating problems that are shared by coaches and players alike: (1) When a player is not ready to pass and rushes his pass anyway, it usually is a poor pass; it may be too hard, too soft or inaccurate. (2) When a player without the ball makes a run to receive a pass but the player with the ball can't pass it (he isn't looking, he is being pressured by a defender, etc.), the running player simply wastes energy.

Youngsters must be taught that offensively there are only two reasons a player without the ball should be running: (1) To receive a pass and (2) to make space.

Finally, remember that this exercise is an excellent conditioner, as well as an exercise to improve skills.

Here are some ways to adapt this exercise:

(1) Have the dribblers pass only with the inside of the foot, then the outside of the foot; then the right foot; then the left foot; then have them alternate feet with each touch.

(2) The passer must pass the ball in less than *four touches* unless he is not ready.

(3) The receiver must also receive with different parts of each foot.

(4) Every third or fourth time a player receives the ball it must be played with one touch.

(5) At the blow of a whistle, the player with the ball attacks the partner and tries to dribble by him.

In between these drill changes have your players rest by passing balls back and forth, tossing air balls to one another, or juggling without running.

4. A variation: The King III. Divide players into groups of three, providing one ball per group, and have them continue to move as they did with single partners. The dribbler may pass to either one of his two partners in the group, who in turn passes to the third partner. Here are a few additional variations:

(1) The first passer passes to a partner who must one-touch it to the third partner.

(2) On the whistle, the partners without the ball attack against the third partner.

(3) Have players make their first two passes 5–10 yards long and the third pass 20 yards long.

(4) Have the receiver let the ball go by him to the second receiver who is running behind (dummy).

FULL TEAM DRILLS

1. King four ball. Bring the entire group together. Inform the players that now they don't have any partners and can pass and receive with anyone. Provide only four balls. As the players pass and move, remind them that they can't yell or say anything. *If they want to receive a pass, they must ask for it by sprinting into a space.*

   2. Keepaway. Divide players into two separate teams. Use one half of the field and one ball. *The object of keepaway is for one team to make ten passes in a row before the other team steals the ball away and makes ten passes in a row.* The passes must be at least five yards and two players cannot make more than three passes between themselves. If one team makes three passes in a row and loses the ball to the other team, they give immediate chase (first rule of defense) to steal the ball back. If they can steal the ball back before the other team completes a pass, they continue counting from three. If one pass has been completed, however, they must go back to zero.
   There are a few variations that can be used for this game too:
   (1) Allow each player only two touches, then three touches, then many touches with the ball.
   (2) Allow players to use only their right foot, left foot, the inside, or the outside of their kicking foot.
   (3) *"Many touches one-touch"*: Teams play keepaway by alternating one-touch and then many touches between players of the same team. This challenges both the passer and the receiver. The player touching the ball many times knows that the teammate he passes to must one-touch the ball, so the ball must be passed with the proper pace. The receiver who is going to receive the pass to be one-touched must know what he is going to do with the ball before he touches. The receiver, therefore, must take "pictures" of the spaces around him, and be aware of defenders and teammates, in order to know where the ball should be passed with one touch.
   (4) In the *"short/short/long game,"* players make two consecutive short passes between 5 and 10 yards and a third pass of at least 20 yards to the other side of the field. One point is given each time the task is completed. Youth soccer players are inclined to bunch

up! We call this *Bee-Hive Soccer.* This drill teaches
your players to move the ball from one side of the field
to the other.

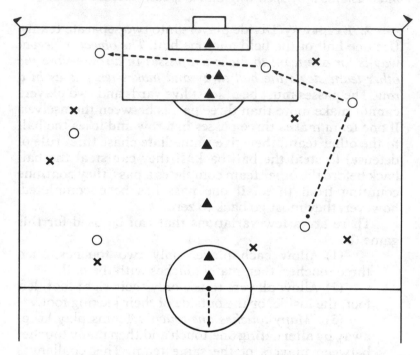

In each of these exercises, variations or gimmicks can
be added to focus on any specific problems your team may
have. Don't be afraid to experiment with the drill changes.
It will help to improve play and should prove to be fun.

You'll find your kids will love this one: *"Go for goal."*
Most of the exercises in this chapter can be modified to
allow the players to "go for goal." For example, if your
team is playing keepaway, yell "Go for goal!" every few
minutes. The team in possession of the ball has ten seconds
in which to score a goal. Use only one goal. The defending
team must quickly *"mark up"* (guard) a man and try to
stop the offensive team from scoring.

Finally, try this for real fun: *"Close your eyes."* Using
the drills mentioned above—keepaway, for example—yell
for the player to close his eyes when he receives a ball.

Now ask him to tell you where two of his teammates (possible receivers) are located. If he can't tell you where they are, it means that he didn't take mental "pictures" of their location before he received the ball. Remind him that the passer must know what he is going to do with the ball before he receives it. Some players will be able to tell you not only where players are but, also, who they are.

At this point in practice talk to your players again and reinforce the importance of not kicking the ball far downfield in a soccer game. That's not soccer, that's kickball.

Let's look at why kickball is popular. Coaches will sometimes play their fastest, most skilled players as forwards. By the time they finish selecting their midfielders and eventually select their backs, the only players left are the smallest, slowest, or least skilled. The players designated as backs, as well as their coach, are petrified that a mistake will occur and the opposing forwards will race in and score a goal. So, the coach instructs them to "kick it out," and the backs become good kickers but very poor soccer players. As a result, the game evolves into one large kickball game played between backs and forwards as the midfielders watch the ball being kicked back and forth over their heads.

What can be done about kickball? First, teach your backs to never kick the ball "out" unless it is in a dangerous position in front of their goal. When this occurs and the backs try to "clear it," the rules are: get height (even if it goes straight up, the goalie can outjump anyone by using his hands); clear the ball to the side; and, finally, get distance. Remind them that if they have time to do all three, they probably had time to settle the ball and pass it out to a teammate and begin to attack. Every time a player kicks the ball "out," the defending team will regain possession half of the time and attack again. So, remember the cardinal rule and teach it to your backs: *Maintain possession of the ball.* Don't give it up. Don't be in a rush to go straight downfield to score a goal. The other team may well have more players back on defense than you do on offense in a certain part of the field. As a result, it may be necessary to attack by passing (not kicking) to another part of the field where your team has numerical superiority.

A final comment to make to your team regarding passing is to reassert the importance of maintaining possession of the ball. Point to the soccer goal on your field and say to your players, "That is the goal we are going for. We don't care how long it takes, but we want to arrive there and with the ball." The team holding the ball the longest usually is the winner. Your team's attitude should be, "Once we get it, we want to keep it."

RECEIVING

Most coaches on every level give little thought to the skill of *getting* the ball as opposed to passing it. We believe you must not only teach the art of receiving but practice it constantly.

Remember the rule: RECEIVING THE BALL IN SOCCER ALWAYS LEADS TO SOMETHING ELSE: MOVING AWAY WITH IT, SHIELDING IT, PASSING IT, OR SHOOTING IT.

The exercises that follow are designed to provide a progression for your players to learn receiving.

1. Stationary reception. In the first exercise, toss balls to each player, who will practice receiving them with the *sole of the foot, instep, inside and outside of the foot, thigh, chest, and head.* After your players are handling most of the tosses comfortably, add pressure to make it more game-related.

Remember, game-related means adding pressure that more closely simulates what your young people will actually experience in a game.

2. Toss and attack. Have the players pair up. One partner tosses the ball. When the receiver touches the ball, the tosser immediately attacks to steal the ball. He has five seconds to pull off the steal. Then the players switch roles. The partners should practice receiving the ball with all parts of the body.

3. Toss and move to space. Next, have the server toss a ball and run into a different space. The receiver must control the ball, then find his partner and pass it to him; or, as a variation, have the receivers one-touch the ball back to the server.

4. Bull in ring. Group your players into fours, combining the sets of pairs already set up. Three of the players each have a ball and form a 15-yard triangle around the fourth player, who is the receiver. The receiver handles a pass from one server, controls it, and returns it with two touches to the same server. Then the receiver takes a pass from the next player, returns it, and finally repeats this drill with the third player. The drill is repeated five times. In the first four rounds the players toss the balls, in turn, to the foot, thigh, chest, and head. In the fifth round the ball is directed anywhere! The players rotate after each completed round.

5. Defender at the D. Group your players in threes around a goal. One player tosses high balls to a receiver who is standing at the D. A defender stands behind the receiver playing low pressure. Low pressure means staying with the player, but not trying to take the ball away. The receiver controls the ball and turns for a shot. As the receiver becomes more proficient, the defender increases pressure, eventually giving the maximum challenge. When the receiver can't make the turn to shoot, he may pass it back to the server.

Remember: THESE EXERCISES DEVELOP RECEIVING SKILLS, BUT ALSO PROMOTE OTHER IMPORTANT SOCCER SKILLS.

DRIBBLING, DRIVING, SHIELDING

Remember the rules:
1. CHANGE SPEED
2. CHANGE DIRECTION
3. KEEP THE HEAD UP

THE ONLY TIME A PLAYER HAS HIS HEAD DOWN IS WHEN HE FIRST TOUCHES THE BALL AND WHEN HE LAST TOUCHES THE BALL.

    1. Creative dribbling. You need to set up a grid for the first dribbling exercise.

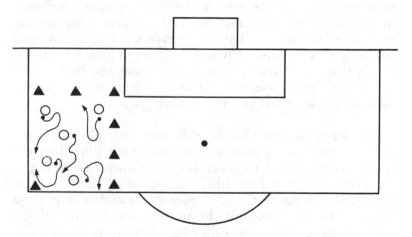

    The size of your grid depends on the number of players you want in the drill and their level of skill. Every player starts with a ball. (If you don't have enough balls to go around, pair up the players, each of the pair taking turns with a ball.) Direct your players to begin dribbling, also telling them you will raise your fist when you want them to stop. This will force your dribblers to keep their heads up.

First, have everyone dribble only with the right foot. Then the left. Then the inside of both feet. Then the outside of both feet. These changes ensure that each player learns to use all parts of the foot. Continually remind everyone to change direction and speed, as well as to dribble with the head up.

2. Whistle drill. Using the same rules, have your players dribble wherever they wish. When you blow the whistle, each player must pick up his/her ball with their hands before you blow the whistle again. Vary the time between the first and second whistle. Then you're controlling the control! Remember, head up!

Use the same grid for Exercise 3 and 4.

3. How many? As the players dribble, raise a number of fingers in the air which the players must perceive immediately by shouting out the number. Change the number of fingers and have the players call it out. As you continue this exercise, tell your players to look for spaces. When you yell "Drive!," they must push the ball into a space and accelerate. After a few seconds, they may resume dribbling until you yell "Drive!" again.

4. King of the hill. In this exercise, players must dribble their ball non-stop. Instruct them that the drill requires each player to knock the other player's ball out of the grid with their feet, like a big game of marbles. Any balls knocked out of the grid may fly no higher than cone height. This ensures that the players use controlled, directed taps to knock out other balls. Whoever remains in the grid with their ball at the end is the winner.

5. Shadow dribbling. Pair up your players for this exercise. One partner takes the ball and dribbles all over the field, executing one-on-one (1-V-1) moves. The other partner follows behind and imitates his moves. This is a good way for players to learn moves from one another. After a minute or so of the activity, have the partners switch responsibilities.

6. 1-V-1/Two goal. The next exercise is one-on-one (1-V-1) through either of two goals. Set up two one-yard-wide goals with cones ten yards apart. Ten yards away, in front of the goals, is an attacker with the ball. The attacker tries to dribble through either of the two goals before the defender steals the ball. The players switch after the attempt.

7. 1-V-1/Two goal counter. The only difference here is that we now have another set of one-yard-wide goals on either side of the attacker. The attacker starts and if the defender steals the ball, he immediately counterattacks and the attacker must play defense.

8. 2-V-2/Two goal. Using the same goal set-up, have players pair up as two attackers and two defenders. Increase the grid area from 10 yards by 10 yards to 15 yards wide by 20 yards long. Now a 2-V-2 situation is presented with the same attack and counterattack rules.

9. Dribbling over the line game. Playing across half of the field, one team tries to score a goal by dribbling over the sideline. The ball cannot be passed but must be dribbled over the line to score a goal.

SHIELDING EXERCISES

1. Five-second shield. In the first exercise, one player stands sideways between the ball and his partner. No one touches the ball. The player closest to the ball tries to shield his partner from the ball for five seconds as the defender tries to step on top of the ball. Encourage the shielding player to stay low, and lean into his partner with his shoulder. After three tries, switch places.

2. 1-V-1 Keepaway. Set up 25 yard by 25 yard grid for the next exercise. Have everyone pair up and stand in the grid. One player is on offense and the other on defense. The exercise begins with the defender trying to steal the ball from the shielding offensive player. If the defender steals the ball from his partner, he gives it back and immediately tries for another steal. After a minute of this, stop and ask for the players who made it through the exercise without having their ball stolen to raise their hand. A variation of this exercise allows the defender to keep the ball if he steals it. Then the offensive player must try to steal it back.

3. Team shielding. In the next exercise, the grid remains the same but the players dribbling the ball must try to shield from everyone. Anyone without a ball can steal from any other player with a ball. In this exercise it's wise to take away a few balls to increase the number of defenders.

4. How many? This last shielding exercise forces the players dribbling the ball to keep their head up and, at the same time, protect it from a defender. Players are paired

up again with one ball. The players shield from one another inside the grid. When a player steals the ball, he keeps it. After a while yell, "How many?" At that moment, the players shielding the ball must look up and shout out the number of fingers being held up. When the shielder is occupied with calling out the number, the defender can attempt a steal.

9
GOALKEEPING

Goalkeepers are very special people, and as a result they need special training to develop.

Unfortunately, many coaches consider their goalkeepers to be defenders only. This just isn't true. Goalkeepers not only *defend* the goal but must *support* all of their teammates and actually start the *attack*. Goalkeepers are *offensive* players, too! It is important to get this attitude across to your goalkeepers and field players.

Goalkeeping is physically and emotionally demanding. It's a good idea, therefore, for all of your team to experience the unique feeling of working in front of the net. Give each player a chance in the goal, and attitudes and perspectives change. Sometimes the best time to switch goalies is right after a goal has been scored against your team. Some field players might be upset with the goalkeeper because "he" gave up the goal. Place the complainer in the goal so he can see how difficult it can be. Remember what was said earlier: no one is allowed to say anything negative to a goalkeeper after a score has occurred. Explain that before the ball got by the goalkeeper, it got by ten other players! The right wing may have lost the ball to a defender and not given immediate chase. The midfielder may not have marked the most dangerous man and enabled a more dangerous player to get free. A back may have run out of control and missed a tackle on the player with the ball. Finally, the ball has reached the goal and the shooter made a great shot. Can the goalkeeper really be blamed for this goal?

1. Patterns. A goalkeeper should keep track of all the goals scored against him. Keeping a log of how the goal was scored, what he did, what the shooter did, and what he should do differently next time (if anything) will help the goalkeeper understand his strengths and weaknesses. Then, in practice, work with him and watch for a pattern to the goals scored against him. Perhaps he needs help with high balls, balls to his left, right, or his agility. Writing down this information *now* will lead to less writing in the *future*.

2. Angle play. Angle play is an extremely crucial part of goalkeeping. Some goalkeepers seem to make one incredible save after another in a game. His play looks spectacular. Fans are cheering his acrobatics. While it is possible that he has the ability to become an incredible goalkeeper, it is also possible that at the moment he is a very poor one. Those incredible saves may just be a result of not playing the angles. Good goalkeepers are excellent at *angle* play, which means narrowing the gap at which the ball can enter the goal.

Playing the angle correctly allows the goalie to place himself directly in front of the player taking a shot.

One way to cut off the shooting angles toward goal is for the goalie to pretend the ball is a flashlight pointed at the goal. The goalie walks out to the flashlight until his shadow covers the goal. He has cut off angles to the left and right. When the ball is being shot from the side of the goal, the goalie should position himself in front of the goal and between the two posts.

A good way to check if the goalie is centered properly is to have a few balls placed in an arc about 18 yards away from the goal.

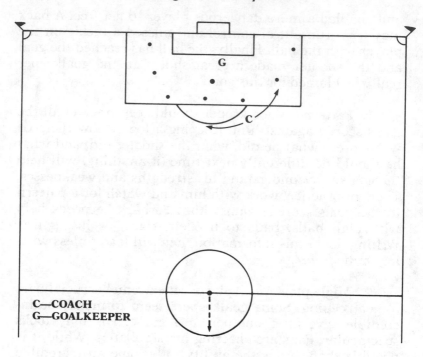

C—COACH
G—GOALKEEPER

The coach should stand behind a ball and have the goalkeeper position himself where he thinks he should be in relation to that ball. Then the goalie can place a towel or his gloves where he was standing and come out to the coach. Both coach and player can now check together to see if the angle was covered, and your keeper will know right away how he did.

To cut off the angle on the high ball, the goalkeeper should play as far in front of the goal as he likes as long as shots on goal can't go over his head and in the goal. How far out each keeper plays will depend on individual speed, quickness, reaction, and judgment. You and the goalies can only find this out in practice. So, shoot balls at them from various distances as they find out just how far out they can come and not get beaten.

3. Catch it. The safest place for a soccer ball is in both of the goalkeeper's hands. The goalkeeper should try to

catch every ball he can. Only if he cannot catch it should he try to deflect it or punch it away. Emphasize to your goalies that they haven't made a save until the soccer ball is in their hands. Knocking the ball down or blocking the shot only constitutes the first part of the save. The good goalie quickly gets back off the ground, finds the ball again, and covers it. (The poor ones will have to turn around and get the ball out of the back of the net.)

As soon as the goalie has the ball in his hands he must start the *attack*. Teach your goalie to look to the opposite side of the field from where the ball was shot. Whenever possible, he should throw or roll the ball out to a field player, which will assure your team a better chance to maintain possession of the ball. When the ball is punted out, the other team will wind up with the ball half the time. There are times, however, when you would want your goalkeeper to punt: if a strong wind or the sun is at his back; if your opponents have very weak backs and you have quicker forwards; if you're losing late in the game; if your opponents are caught up on attack and your deepest man has a 1-V-1 with a back; or if your backs are weak and having trouble passing the ball and building the attack.

4. Communication. The goalie must communicate with his field players; like a baseball catcher, he is the only player with the entire game in front of him and must let his teammates know what he sees. When the goalkeeper wants the ball he must scream "keeper" and demand it. When a ball is cleared out of the goal area, he must yell for his teammates to push out. (This action will catch teams offside.) He must yell for teammates to mark up (guard) a man when under attack. He must alert his teammates if they are backing up into the goal and screening him from the shot.

5. High balls. Your goalkeeper must at least be able to dominate the 6-yard goal area. As he develops confidence and skill he will control a greater area. High balls can be a problem for some goalkeepers. When explaining how a

goalie should jump to catch a ball, tell him to pretend he is jumping as if taking a basketball to dunk with both hands. He should swing one knee up in front of his waist to give lift. Bringing the knee up will also give protection to his ribs from a charging forward.

6. Restarts. Restarts (free kicks, corner kicks, throw-ins) are very dangerous situations and must have everyone's undivided attention, especially the goalkeeper's. When your team is setting up its defensive wall, the goalie must yell out the number of people needed. A defensive wall is just what it says: A wall of stationary players designed to present an obstacle to the opposing player taking a free kick.

If your opposition is not attempting a shot, there is no reason to have a wall. Once the goalkeeper calls for the number of players he wants in the wall, set it up first by lining up the tallest player with the near post. He should not line up the ball, as a shot may be taken while he is occupied. Let a midfielder do it. If the opposition is taking a corner kick, get two players, one on each post, to cover the goal in the event the goalie must come out of goal to catch the ball. Don't put a back on the post. Coaches do this all the time. Isn't it silly to have your best defenders guard a post and your worst defenders, the forwards, guard the opposition's best players?

If the opposition has a throw-in in your defensive third of the field, they may have a player who can reach the goal. Remember: the ball cannot be thrown into the goal. It must touch someone, goalkeepers included, before it can count as a goal. Don't forget that the offensive team can't be offside when the ball is thrown in.

Of course, the main advantage goalkeepers maintain over field players is that they can use their hands, but remember that this advantage exists only in the penalty area.

When a shot is taken on goal, the goalie must learn to catch the ball in both hands.

The fingers should be spread over as wide an area as possible and "give" as the ball hits his hands.

Whenever possible, the goalkeeper should move his body behind the ball as well, which gives added protection on dropped or deflected catches. When playing shots in his area, the goalie should position himself behind the ball, catch it, and then clutch it to his body.

When catching balls directed between the chest and knees, use a basket catch. Stand with palms of hands facing up and arms parallel. Catch the ball with both hands, arms against the body. Lean slightly forward and catch with the hands first, and then trap in the body.

On rolling shots he should stand with feet close enough together that the ball can't slip through.

The player should hold palms open toward the ball with fingers pointing to the ground. As the catch is made, the player brings the ball up to the chest and clutches it.

7. Delivering the ball—starting the attack. All goal-keepers must learn to throw and punt. As previously mentioned, there are times when the goalkeeper should punt the ball. Whenever a punt is taken, however, the other team will gain possession half of the time. Whenever possible, the goalie should throw the ball to a teammate because it is easier to control and will help your team maintain possession. Your goalie may need both hands to bring the soccer ball back to the throwing position.

As he brings the ball over the throwing shoulder, he should spread his fingers, step forward and throw. Teach him to snap his hand straight down on the follow-through as if he were throwing a fast ball.

When your goalie practices punting, have him concentrate first of all on striking the center of the ball on the laces. Then these are the steps: (1) Point the toe and lock the ankle. (2) Drop the ball on the foot—don't throw it in the air and hope to kick it.

Have your goalies practice this technique by standing 10 yards apart and punting back and forth. Gradually move them apart until they are punting for distance. This is also good practice for catching high balls.

You can devise any number of exercises for the goalkeeper. He can throw balls up in the air to himself, then sit down, or kneel, roll, or do a push-up, quickly get up and catch the ball. Anything that forces him to move and catch balls from different positions and angles is great. It will help his agility and quickness and so make him a better goalkeeper.

As stated, the goalkeeper is a special player. He is also an equal member of your team and should be treated as such. The coach must find ways each practice to incorporate him into the training session. The goalie must learn his teammates' strengths and weaknesses, and they, his. It is important to incorporate him into the various shooting exercises and offensive and defensive tactical exercises that have been discussed.

10
OFFENSIVE
TACTICS

Soccer is a game of opposites. The offensive team stretches itself across the field to gain width and depth as a team. The defensive team tries to condense itself. At the same time the attackers are trying to outnumber and penetrate the defense, their opponents are trying to get more players back to defend their goal. A creative offense can overrun and penetrate the defense, as players improvise to find a way to get the ball into the net.

Before you as a coach can introduce any team tactics, individual skills must be taught to every field player. Each player must be able to dribble, shield, pass, receive, and shoot. When individual skills have been developed at game speed, team tactics can be introduced successfully.

Attacking. When attacking, the player with the ball should face his offensive goal and look for the *deepest* man. If he can play a ball to that player, he should. This *penetration pass* cuts through the defense and immediately leaves a pack of defenders behind the ball. If it is too risky to play a ball directly forward, the player should look to play a ball *diagonally*. If this is also too risky, your player must look to pass a square ball out to the side or behind him to a supporting player. Any pass played square or backward is considered a *possession pass*. Since penetration passes are risky, always have your offense possess the ball until it can find a weaker area to attack. Your most important concern as a coach is for your guys or gals to maintain possession of the ball. Remember: in a soccer game, one team plays soccer and the other team chases. If you give up the ball, you have to chase.

1-V-1 OFFENSIVE EXERCISES

Let's look at some exercises for one-on-one attack.

Your attacking players must have complementary moves to beat defenders to the right and to the left. They can attack much more quickly *by using one foot*. Utilizing the inside and outside of the same foot, a player can make head, shoulder, hip and leg feints without even touching the ball! The ball can do the work as the dribbler fakes—with his head up!—watching to see which way the defender leans.

1. Cone tag. A good way to practice this is to line up your players and place one defender 10 yards away in front of two cones that are 5 yards apart. The defender's job is to tag the attacker with two hands. The attacker has five seconds to try to run through the cones without being tagged. *No* balls are used. After each kid attacks, he becomes the defender. By playing without a ball, your players will learn all sorts of fakes with the head, shoulders, hips, and legs. When a player beats the defender by running to one side, ask him why he ran to that side. He will say that he saw the defender lean the opposite way. And how did he know? He had his head up! Now try the same drill with the ball. Instruct your players to let the ball do the work, letting it roll as they feint keeping their head up and using one foot.

2. The Step-over. There are two ways to feint and step over a ball:

(1) The player's foot may pass over the ball from

the outside in; or (2) the player's foot may pass over the ball from the inside out.

Outside In: If the player steps over the ball with his right foot by stepping toward the left foot, he has stepped from the outside in.

Inside Out: If the player steps over the ball with his right foot going *away* from his left foot, he is stepping from the inside out.

A simple way for players to attack 1-V-1 is to dribble at the defender, feint by stepping over the ball with the right foot from the inside out. Lean in that direction and then use the outside of your left foot to dribble by the defender to your left. The same can be done by feinting with the left and going to the right.

Another 1-V-1 move is a *scissor*. If your players are able to do the last move, they are halfway there. Have them attack the defender, feint by stepping over from the inside out at the left, then inside out at the right, and then use the outside of the left foot to accelerate by the defender to the left. What they have done is two stepover moves from the inside out. Be aware that with the scissor more distance is necessary between the attacker and the defender, as the move takes longer. With head kept up, they will see the defender, start it sooner, and not fall over in a tangle of feet and legs!

Two advanced 1-V-1 moves that result in both a change of speed and direction are the *reverse dribble* and the *behind-the-leg dribble*. Both of these moves are similar to their basketball counterparts. Your players can use the reverse dribble effectively when the attacking player is forced to one side. If the attacking player is moving to the right, he accelerates to force the defender to commit himself. Then the dribbler steps between the ball and defender, and shields turning sideways. Using the outside of his right foot, the attacker curls his foot around the ball and pulls it back in the reverse direction. The behind-the-leg move is like the behind-the-back dribble in basketball. In soccer, the dribbler starts to one side and then uses the inside of his foot to pass the ball behind the supporting leg.

The most important thing to teach your players about beating any defender is that the defender will only remain "beaten" for a moment. Too often an attacker will beat a defender and then casually dribble off, only to have the defender give immediate chase and steal the ball back. Then the attacker has to beat the same defender again. Whenever the attacker beats a defender, *he must accelerate quickly away from the opponent.*

To practice any of these moves, have your players try them first *without* defenders. Then pair them up and tell the defender to play 50 percent defense and lean in a certain direction. The attacker must have his head up and go in the opposite direction. Finally, build up the pressure to game conditions. A team game of keepaway is fun with the restriction that a player cannot pass the ball to a teammate until he has beaten a defender.

2-V-1 OFFENSIVE EXERCISES

When your players get a 2-V-1 situation going (two attackers and one defender), your team has achieved the ideal offensive situation: *NUMERICAL SUPERIORITY.* This allows your team to at least penetrate the opponent's defense and perhaps get a shot on goal.

For the first drill set up a 10 yard by 10 yard practice area. Have one player positioned as a defender and stand between two cones about eight yards from the two attackers.

There are three pairs of attackers in two lines. The attackers alternate and the defender plays defense for three turns. One pair starts with the ball and the player with the ball goes directly at the defender. Some youngsters think they will lose the ball to the defender but *the attacker's attitude must be that they are in charge and the defender is in trouble.* As each player attacks, he must be thinking one of two things: (1) fake a pass to his teammate and dribble past the defender, or (2) fake dribbling the ball by the defender, drawing the defender's attention, and passing to his teammate.

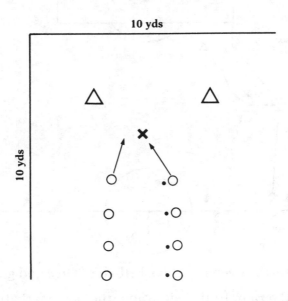

The positioning of the receiving player is extremely important. He must try to stay a yard back of the attacker for three reasons: (1) If he runs too far ahead in the attacking third of the field, he may be offside. (2) If the receiver is at midfield, and not offside, another defender will probably be giving cover (support) and step up to intercept the pass. (If you watch a soccer game, you will notice that 2-V-2 is the usual situation wherever the ball is.) (3) To avoid having the defender cut off the passing angle by stepping forward with his leg.

MISCELLANEOUS EXERCISES

1. Wall pass—soccer's "Give and go". In this 2-V-1 exercise, the passer plays the ball to the receiver and gets a return pass as he runs behind the defender.

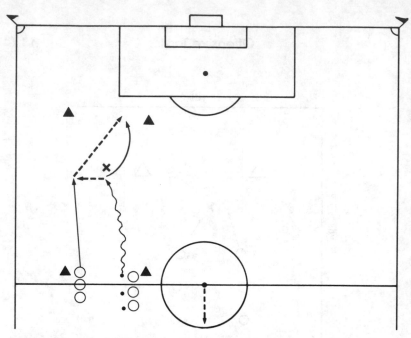

This is soccer's version of basketball's "Give and go."

2. Overlap. In this situation, the play starts by passing the ball directly to the receiver. The passer then runs around the receiver and the receiver dribbles diagonally at the defender. The receiver keys the defender and either passes it back to the original passer or keeps the ball and dribbles past.

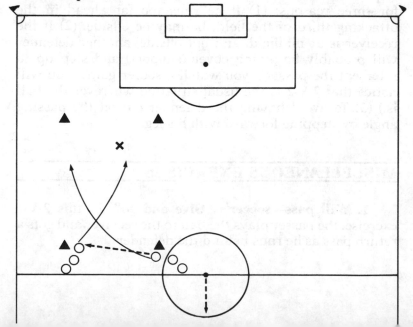

3. Takeover. Here the passer dribbles across in front of the defender as the receiver runs behind his teammate.

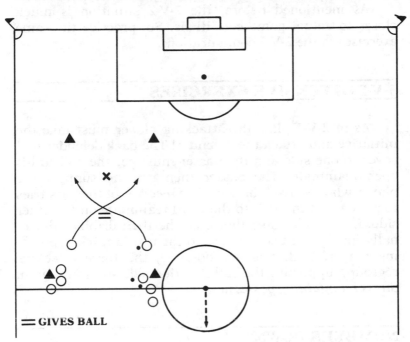

= GIVES BALL

The ball is exchanged as players change possession, using right foot to right foot or left foot to left foot. In this way, a collision is avoided.

4. Diagonal. Your team can also attack 2-V-1 by directing a receiver to make a diagonal run behind the defender. If the defender goes with the receiver, the passer continues unmolested. If the defender covers the passer, he passes to the receiver. The receiver must not allow the defender to stand in the passing lane between the passer and receiver.

Now you must develop these 2-V-1 tactics in a more gamelike situation. Achieve this with a simple exercise where your players attack two on one and finish with a shot on goal. Follow this exercise by adding another goal for the defender to counter the attack. Finally, have the kids play a small-sided game of 4-V-4 or 5-V-5 and give points every time a team successfully completes a 2-V-1.

As mentioned before, the 2-V-2 situation is much closer to actual game conditions. So, practice the same exercises in the 2-V-2 configuration.

3-V-2 OFFENSIVE EXERCISES

As in 2-V-1 play, the attacking player must take the initiative and attack the defender! The back defender will cover to one side and the passer must get the ball to his open teammate. The passer then runs to support the player who received the ball. The receiver of the pass tries to pass a ball through to the third teammate on the other side. If he can't make that pass, he then dribbles diagonally inside and tries to pass to the overlapping supporting player. If that is not possible, the three attackers regroup, supporting the ball on either side and start again. *Stress maintaining possession.*

NUMBERS DOWN

In most of these exercises, your offense has played with numerical superiority. While this does occur in soccer games, more often the defense outnumbers the offense in specific play situations. So it is important to drill your offense in "numbers down" exercises. For example, take your players to the offensive third of the field. Have three players attack four defenders and try to develop a shot on goal. If the defense steals the ball, give the attackers ten seconds to steal the ball back. If the defense maintains possession for ten seconds, then rotate in three new attackers. This exercise can also be played in 4-V-5, 5-V-6, or 6-V-7 situations to mimic game conditions.

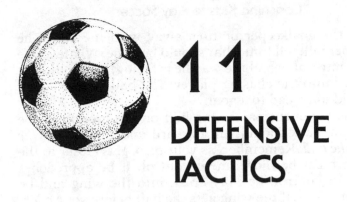

11
DEFENSIVE TACTICS

As we said earlier, soccer is a game of opposites. While attackers try to stretch the defense, the defense condenses itself to defend the most dangerous area which is in front of the goal. (At higher levels of play, players will learn to defend areas all over the field as they *become* dangerous. Your defensive goal area is not very dangerous if your opponents have the ball 10 yards in front of their goal.) Attackers will try to get more players in an area than there are defenders, while defenders of course will try to out-number the attackers. When the opposing team has pene-trated your defensive third of the field, they will try to be creative and improvise. Your defenders should try to cut off play options for the attackers. This will make the attacker's moves more predictable and easier to handle.

Assume that you have just assigned a youngster to play left back. It's the first time he has played this position. Apprehensive, he asks what he should do. Calmly tell him to mark the right wing. Identify that player and explain that he should first stay between the wing and the goal (goalside). Make certain he plays far enough away from the wing so if a ball is kicked over his head toward the goal, he won't be outraced to the ball. If his opponent does make a long kick, all your player should do is pass the ball back to the goalkeeper or turn away with the ball. The goalkeeper will tell him what should be done. Whatever he does, he must play ball the way he is facing. He should not turn back into the chasing player. The ball can be stolen easily and may lead to a goal.

If his opponent passes the ball on the ground to the wing, your back should run forward and try to *beat the wing to the ball*. Remember, as your back gets closer to the wing, he must be more under control. If he approaches him out of control, he may crash into the wing and be called for a foul. If the wing gets the ball before your back, he may use the back's speed and aggressiveness against him and fake by him. If the wing beats your back to the ball, *don't let the wing turn with the ball*. He cannot pass the ball forward or take a shot if your back does not allow him to turn. The wing will be forced to pass the ball back in the direction of his own goal. This will give the other defenders time to get back on defense. The back should try to poke the ball away from the wing when he is behind him.

Let's pretend that the wing was able to turn with the ball. Maybe the back slipped. Now the wing faces your back and begins to attack. If the back plays in front of the wing, he can beat him to the left, right, or through the legs. He is at the wing's mercy because he has no idea which way he will attack. The back should try to force the wing in one direction—to the sideline. To do this he just has to move to the inside of the field. This accomplishes a number of things: The wing can only move in one direction—to the outside. As the wing dribbles down the field, his shooting angle becomes worse and he has little chance to score. With the ball at the sideline, and not the middle, other defenders have a much easier task marking their men. They can slide toward the ball and create a defensive triangle between the ball, their opponent, and themselves. Since the ball can only be passed in one direction, your players won't be deceived and with proper positioning can handle the pass safely.

Forwards must learn to play defense: If a forward loses the ball on attack, he must be the first person back on defense.

As the forwards chase the ball from behind, midfielders run back to get between the goal and their opponents. Everyone marks a man. To give your defense time to prepare, the player who pressures the ball should delay the attack by *jockeying* his opponent. (Jockeying is a delaying tactic which results from a player "bothering" the man with the ball, forcing him to slow down and/or move to one side or another.) His teammates now have time to get back on defense and mark their men. Defenders must pick up the most dangerous man first. It's usually obvious who that is. If one attacking player is 40 yards from the goal and another attacker is 20 yards away, guess who's more dangerous! Make this point very clear to your players.

EXERCISES TO DEVELOP DEFENSE

1. 1-V-1 five-second drill. Divide your team, lining up half of the players 40 yards from the goal, each player with a ball. The other half of the team acts as defenders, lined up on one side of a goal post. The exercise begins when the first defender runs out from the goal. When the first player in the attacking line sees the defender run, he begins to attack 1-V-1, and the attacker has five seconds to score. The defender should force the attacker to one side and not allow him to turn back.

2. Can't-turn drill. Set up two grids, 10 yards by 20 yards, side by side. Split the team in half so that each group may do the same exercise in one grid. Two players are in the center of the grid, and two players, passers, stand at each end of the grid with two balls each.

The object of the exercise is for one player in the grid to receive a ball, turn with it, and pass the ball to the player on the other side. The defensive objective is to beat the offensive player to the ball. If he can't beat him to the ball, he does not allow him to turn. The offensive player can pass the ball back the way he is facing and try to get free again. If the defender steals the ball or knocks it out of

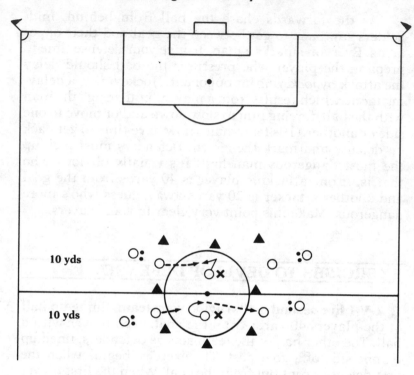

the grid, he becomes the new offensive player as the players switch roles. Limit the time to about 30–45 seconds. After the players have had a few opportunities, combine both groups and do the same exercise with 2-V-2 in the entire grid area. This exercise will help develop the player's ability to give cover and create a defensive triangle when not pressuring the ball.

3. 3-V-3 midfield drill. Set up three lines with a center forward, right wing, and left wing positioned, with defenders on each.

Defenders are not allowed to steal the ball, only position themselves. Have the center forward start with the ball. He passes it to a wing and moves slightly toward him. The wing passes it back and the center forward passes it to the other wing and moves toward him. The attackers move

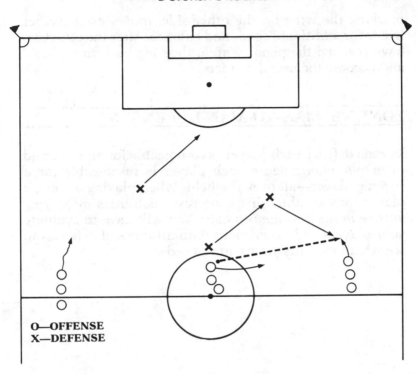

O—OFFENSE
X—DEFENSE

forward slowly and should reach the penalty area by the
time the ball has changed direction about three times.
When the center forward has the ball, a defender covers
him. The outside defenders marking the wings move inside
at a 45-degree angle toward the central defender. By sliding toward the middle, the outside defenders create a
defensive triangle with the ball, their man, and themselves. This position gives the outside defender a head
start on the wing if the wing were to try to run inside him
for a *through ball* (a pass made between defenders to a
teammate moving into space). By moving inside, the outside defender also gives cover to his teammate to the
inside if he is beaten. Remember, after a pass is made to a
wing, your defenders must adjust and pressure the ball,
with your central defender sliding to the ball at a 45-
degree angle and giving cover to the wing. The defender,

marking the wing on the other side, moves even farther inside for additional cover and balance. After the attackers have reached the penalty area, they jog back to midfield and become the new defenders.

ZONE VS. MAN-TO-MAN DEFENSES

In zone defense each player is responsible for an *area,* and in *man-to-man* defense each player is responsible for a specific player—all over the field. When playing a zone, a player may combine his zone responsibilities *by playing anyone in his area man to man.* You will have to evaluate your players and experiment with all types of defenses to see what best suits your team's needs.

12

RESTARTS

During the game, a referee may stop play for a number of reasons. The act of putting the ball back into play is called a *restart*. Because restarts are so important to the game, this entire chapter deals with them.

THROW-IN—When the ball goes over the touch line (sideline), the team that touched it last loses possession. The other team now throws the ball back into play, one teammate to another. The player throwing the ball must toss with two hands (forming a "w" with thumbs and index finger). Players cannot throw the ball directly into the goal; it must touch someone else first. Remember, the offensive team can't be offside on a throw-in.

GOAL KICK—If an offensive player last touched the ball before it crossed the goal line, the opposing team is awarded a goal kick. Anyone on the defending team can take a goal kick. It must be taken from the ground any-where within half of the 6-yard goal area, depending on the half of the goal line that the ball went over. Before anyone else can touch the ball after the goal kick, it must come completely out of the penalty area.

CORNER KICK—If the ball was last touched by a defender before going over the goal line, a corner kick is awarded to the opposing team, within the corner arch on the side of the field where the ball crossed the goal line.

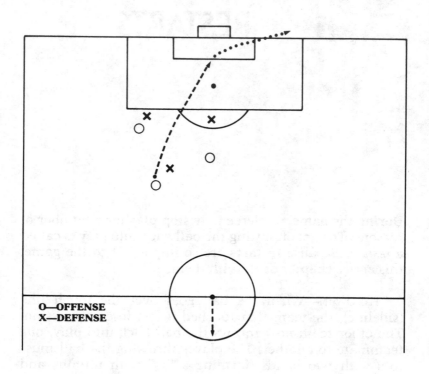

O—OFFENSE
X—DEFENSE

All defensive players must stand at least 10 yards from the ball.

SHORT CORNER—The short corner play can be run a number of ways. Have one player pass the ball to a teammate and then run toward the goal (overlap). The two offensive players go 2-V-1 against the first covering defender. If the ball is passed to the overlapping player, he can shoot. Or the first player can dribble with the ball along the goal line and cross the ball. Remind your players that this is a better choice if the field is very wide or the player making the corner kick can't reach the goal. Here is one last version of the short corner kick: player runs out from the goal, receives the corner kicker's pass, and returns it to him as he moves toward the goal.

CORNER KICK STRATEGY—If you have some taller players on your team, you may want to practice driving high corner kick passes. If your players are smaller, hard low-driving corner kicks will set up better chances on goal. This pass is easily deflected to teammates and may lead to confusion in front of the goal. (Many teams will put a player in front of the goalie to run toward the ball. Your other players should make runs to the near post, far post, and central positions. Still others should stand near the D and try to shoot back any balls headed away from the goal.)

Teach your kids these strategies on how to *defend corner kicks:*

1. Put one player on each post to defend the goal in case the goalkeeper must come out to make a save. Have your other players mark men according to size, speed, or ability.

2. Spread your team into a zone, making each player responsible for an area. Position four players along the 6-yard line. Place a few more around the penalty spot and maybe another out by the corner kicker. The man defending the kicker should block or distract the kicker and help defend the short corner.

3. You can also defend the corner kick this way: have some players play zone and a few mark the best players man to man. Judge which method works best for your team, based on your opponent and your own skills and abilities.

FREE KICK—There are two kinds of free kicks—direct and indirect. (These break down into restarts in shooting distance and out-of-shooting distance, but you should consult the rules section to see what foul results in what kick.) When the opposing team is within shooting distance, set up your defense in a wall to block the part of the goal the goalkeeper leaves empty while he plays the opponent's direct kick. Your goalkeeper must handle balls kicked around or over the wall. The offense will try to put the ball in play immediately before a wall can be set up. The kicking player will either take a shot on goal (direct), or pass to a teammate for a shot (indirect).

Your goalkeeper should call out the number of players needed in the wall and a field player should line everyone up with the near post. When your team has set the wall, the player who lined it up should mark any unmarked player. If everyone is marked, he should give chase to any ball passed for a shot or overlap. Keep your backs out of the wall, if possible. Usually they are your best defenders and will be more effective marking a player. If your opponent is out of shooting distance, most will try to chip the ball in front of the goal. In this situation defensive players should mark a man and hold at the 18-yard line; any ball chipped into the goal area can be handled by the goalkeeper as the defenders cover the attacking players. Defenders must stay with their men until the ball is safely in the goalkeeper's hands.

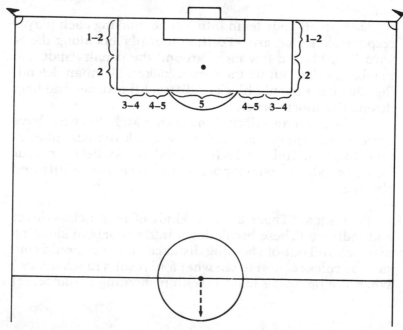

When your team gets a free kick, use the strengths of individual players to determine what you want to try. Do you have one or two swift players who can outrace their man to a spot in front of the goal? Do you have a good passer who can chip over defenders to that spot? Do you have a player who is able to bend balls over or around a wall? Don't be afraid to be a little deceptive—designing these "set pieces" in practice will make for more productive free kicks in games.

PENALTY KICK—Penalty kicks are high-percentage shots and should be as automatic as an extra point in football. The penalty spot is 12 yards away from the goal. During the kick the goalkeeper must have his heels on the line and cannot move until the ball is kicked. Everyone except the shooter must be out of the penalty area and penalty arch (D). The shooter chooses a side and tries to place the ball within 3 feet of that post. Many players will take a penalty kick using a push pass. Done with the inside of the foot, this shot is more accurate than an instep kick and can still be struck powerfully enough to beat the goalkeeper. At higher levels of play, goalkeepers will guess the side the player is shooting for and dive in that direction. At the youth level it is probably more realistic for the goalie to wait until the ball is shot and then react.

13

SYSTEMS OF PLAY (Where Do I Play, Coach?)

Regardless of where a youngster plays, he must understand that when his team has the ball he is on offense, and when the opponent has the ball he is on defense.

A team does not win or lose because it plays a particular system. The skill with which individual players and the team as a whole execute specific techniques and tactics determines who plays well and usually wins . . . or who plays less well and usually loses. Outstanding technique will make any system a successful one.

Before choosing a system for your team, analyze your players. What are their strengths and weaknesses? After careful consideration, determine who should play where so that everyone is matched to the most appropriate or practical position. Then choose a system.

Most team systems start with a minimum of four backs (plus goalkeeper), two midfielders, and two forwards. That leaves two players. Adding these to the backfield would weigh down your defense. Placing both of them as forwards would make you strong offensively, but too weak at midfield. Are the two midfielders strong enough to cover midfield by themselves? It might be wise to start out with three midfielders and three forwards until you really know your players. In this 4-3-3 system (always number from the back forward), you must have a back who reads the game very well, is a good header, and has good skills. Play him as a SWEEPER—a free back who doesn't have to mark anyone. The three remaining backs will mark your opponent's center forward and two wings. If you have a skilled, attack-oriented player at midfield, you should play him as an attacking midfielder and leave the other mid-fielders to cover for him and play more defensively. Do you have a forward who can beat defenders 1-V-1 and can cross a ball well? Perhaps he can play as a wing. Make sure to have him play on the side of your opponent's weakest back, once you determine who it is. This will create a mismatch to your advantage.

Here are a few diagrams to help you picture the various systems of play:

4-3-3- SYSTEM

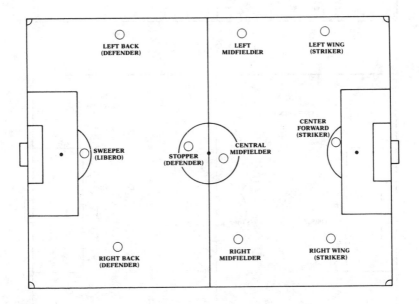

4-4-2 SYSTEM

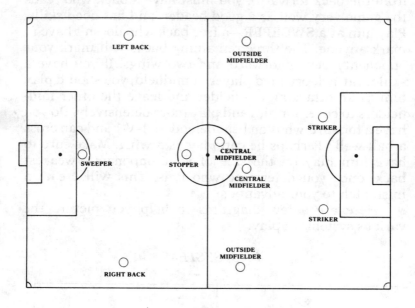

4-2-4 SYSTEM

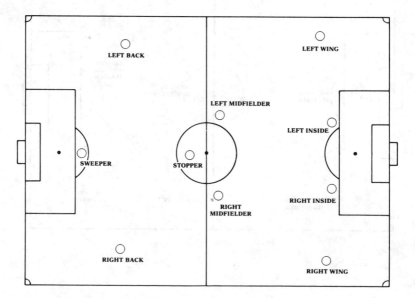

14
PRE-GAME CHECK LIST

Before the practice or game ever begins, it is important to make sure you have everything necessary to run the game efficiently. Using our pre-game check list will help you remember to bring the things needed for practice, but this doesn't mean that *you* have to bring everything. If you have an assistant or two, they can help; parents are often happy to bring what they can. Check the medical kit beforehand to make certain you have sufficient supplies—band aids, gauze pads, Ace bandages, etc.

(You might want to remove this list from the book or copy it and attach it to your clipboard.)

Our Pre-Game Check List

1. Soccer Balls
2. Cones, corner flags
3. Scorebook—with clipboard and two pencils
4. Pinnies—or different-colored shirts—in case the other team shows up with the same uniform
5. Medical Kit—with emergency phone number(s) and two quarters taped inside*

*Youth-league soccer is often played on fields that aren't near telephones. In case of emergency you should *know* the location of the nearest phone and the numbers to call for police and ambulance. Many coaches designate a parent as the "runner" to the phone if a bad injury occurs.

6. Shinguards—two pair for the kids who forget them
7. Cooler-fill with bags of ice, unless you have instant ice packs
8. Rule book
9. Horn or whistle for substitutions
10. Roster of your players, their parents or guardians, and phone numbers

15
PRACTICE AND PRE-GAME WARM-UP ROUTINE

Before any practice or game you must warm up your players and stretch their playing muscles. Stretching will help prevent injuries and improve flexibility. Concentrate on the muscles specifically used often in soccer. Each player should stretch until it feels a bit uncomfortable, then hold back slightly. The stretch should be held about 8 seconds. No bouncing—just hold the stretch.

Stretching the Hamstrings (back of leg); Bend over at the waist with crossed legs and touch the toes.

Back Stretch: With legs apart, look as far over one shoulder as you can. Then twist the body in that direction and hold for 8 seconds.

Quadriceps Stretch (front of thigh): Stand on one leg and pull the other foot behind as the knee is bent. Focus the eyes on a blade of grass or an object on the ground to help maintain balance, or just lean on a friend.

Groin: Stretch sitting down and place the soles of the feet together with knees to the sides. Lean forward and try to press down lightly on the knees.

138

Be aware that each youngster is different and that some players will be more flexible than others. Explain to the youngsters that if they do not feel sufficiently warmed up at the end of the warm-up period, they may go ahead and continue to stretch some more. Spend extra time stretching muscle groups you plan to stress during practice. If you're going to concentrate on shooting, for example, do extra stretching for legs and back.

After light stretching, each player should do some running. Be sure to lead the players through all the types of running they will use in a game—forward, backward, sideways (heel-clickers). Finish by hopping and then jumping to head an imaginary ball. After this type of running, do exercises *to increase circulation and body temperature* to warm up the muscles: sit-ups, push-ups, "Jumping Jacks."

These exercises also improve the players strength and fitness. Vary the exercises, the number of exercises, and whenever possible, use a ball when warming up to avoid boredom and promote enthusiasm. The more familiar a player is with the ball, the more relaxed he will be with it. Besides, it's more fun!

As important as the warm-up is the cool-down, which helps minimize muscle soreness. The cool-down aids circulation in and clears waste products from the muscles. Light stretching again will help the cool-down process and help prevent the tightening of muscles that usually results from vigorous exercise.

Prior to a game, it is also important to warm up and stretch, but it is not necessary to try to build strength prior to the game by doing push-ups or sit-ups. Instead, pair the kids up. Have them warm up with a partner and a ball, using all the techniques they will use in the game. Have them imagine certain game situations and act them out— shooting at their partner as if he were the goal, taking goal kicks, heading the ball, taking a corner kick. Adding a third player to your warm-up can make it more creative. Then bring the team together and practice some tactics, both offensive and defense. Try a 3-V-2 on goal. After this exercise, let your team do a few shooting drills. When the whistle blows, you are ready.

SOME CONCLUDING THOUGHTS

If you've read this book from start to finish, we are confident that you have a good solid base on which to build your soccer team. We hope you now have a feel for teaching the fundamentals of the game and helping your players apply them.

If you have used this book as another source of information about soccer, we know you have found some nuggets—some gems—with which to prepare your team more effectively for this wonderful game.

No matter what the reason, we hope you've enjoyed this book and will refer to it often. Soccer has been called "the beautiful game" by the legendary Pelé. We agree and feel that you too are beautiful for being part of it.

Good luck, Coach. We've been pleased to help.

GLOSSARY

(Source: *Schools Programme Manual*, Ontario Soccer Association)

Angle, Narrowing the: When defenders, especially the goalkeeper, move closer to the ball in order to reduce passing or shooting angles.

Cross, Diagonal: Usually played in the offensive third of the field; a ball played forward from right to left or left to right.

Cross, Far Post: A pass made to the goal post farthest from the point from which the ball was kicked.

Cross, Near Post: A pass made to the goal post nearest from the point where the ball was kicked.

Defense, Back of: The space between the goalkeeper and the defender nearest to him.

Dribble: Possessing the ball with short touches of the feet.

Driving: Running with the ball by pushing it ahead into spaces and moving after it.

Dummy: When the receiver of a pass feints touching the ball and lets it run by him to a teammate running behind.

Feint: A fake; can be applied to kicking or moving.

Flight: The trajectory of the ball.

Goal side of the ball: The defensive player's position between the player he is marking and the goal he is defending.

Instep: The upper surface of the foot; the laces.

Lofted drive: A powerful kick with the instep driving through the bottom half of the ball.

Marking man to man: Defense which requires each of your players to play man to man against an opponent.

Pass, Chip: A pass made by stabbing at the bottom of the ball, causing it to go in the air with backspin.

Pass, Flick: A pass made by an outward rotation of the kicking foot, causing contact with the outside of the foot.

Pass, Push: The most used pass in soccer. Ball is struck with the inside of the foot.

Pass, Volley: A pass made by making contact with the ball before it hits the ground.

Pass, Wall: A pass between two players where the receiver passes the ball right back to the passer at a similar angle at which he received it.

Play, Take-over: Crossing motion by two attacking players in which they exchange the ball with the same foot.

Play, One-touch: Passing the ball without first controlling it.

Player, Supporting: Usually a teammate behind the ball, in a position to receive a pass.

Receiving: Controlling the ball by withdrawing the surface used to make contact with it.

Redirecting: Altering the angle and flight of the ball in one movement.

Run, Overlap: The movement of an attacking player from a position behind the ball, around the player with the ball, to a position ahead of the ball.

Space, Creating: Increasing distance between yourself and a teammate, to the side, in front of, or behind opponents.

Tackle: A challenge to win the ball from an opponent.

Thirds of the field: Roughly 35-yard sections of the field. Thirds are designated the defending, the middle, and the attacking.

Turning an opponent: Causing an opponent to turn because you have either played the ball past him or run past him.

Turning with the ball: The act of receiving the ball when facing your goal, then turning with the ball to face the opponent's goal.

GENERAL RESOURCES

Many of the drills and skill descriptions contained herein derive from other coaches and books. Further resources containing information about coaching children and soccer follow:

American Coaching Effectiveness Program. Champaign, Illinois: U. of Chicago.

Canadian Soccer Association, Toronto, Canada; Ontario Soccer Association. *Schools Programme Manual. Level I, II, III Coaching Manuals.*

United States Soccer Federation, Colorado Springs, Colorado. *The Official Soccer Book of the USSF:* Walt Chyzowych. *Coaches Manual:* Robert McNulty and Leonard Lucenko.

Soccer Skills and Tactics. Ken Jones and Pat Welton. New York: Crown, 1976.

Winning Soccer. A. Miller and Norm Wingert. Chicago: Regnery, 1975.